D1576661

C334013825

ALL IN THE
FOOD

A Word from Dr Frank Cullen, Head of School

Celebrating 75 years of culinary excellence, *All in the Food* captures the essence of Cathal Brugha Street, which began as a domestic science cookery school in 1941, and is today our School of Culinary Arts and Food Technology, DIT. The book is testament to the dedication of all those who, over the years, have worked to achieve and maintain international standards in food and drinks education.

Many of our graduates, including Darina Allen, Kevin Thornton and Keelan Higgs, have gone on to celebrated status as Michelin star chefs, award-winning bakers, and restaurant, hospitality and industry professionals. Along with staff and supporters of the school, such as Michel Roux OBE, Paul Kelly and Ross Lewis, they have kindly contributed to *All in the Food*, with their delicious, easy-to-make recipes for dining at home and some restaurant-quality dishes for the more experienced cook to try.

Packed with photographs, top tips on food, drink and entertaining, and peppered with fascinating facts about the school's development through the years, *All in the Food* offers a tantalising mix of recipes, glimpses into the school's past and aspirations for the future.

With the 75th anniversary, the school felt that it was important to showcase all the talented and inspiring people associated with the school. A publication of this kind could not materialise without the support of the publishers The O'Brien Press, the School of Culinary Arts and Food Technology management team and staff members plus the many contributors featured in this book. We thank you all sincerely. As Head of School, I am proud to present a book developed by such a group of skilled culinary arts, food science, bakery, beverage, and hospitality professionals for your enjoyment.

Dr Frank Cullen

Head of School of Culinary Arts and Food Technology,

Dublin Institute of Technology,

Cathal Brugha Street, Dublin

ALL IN THE FOOD

75 YEARS OF CATHAL BRUGHA STREET
Celebrating Irish Culinary Excellence

School of Culinary Arts and Food Technology,
Dublin Institute of Technology

THE O'BRIEN PRESS
DUBLIN

First published 2016 by
The O'Brien Press Ltd,
12 Terenure Road East, Rathgar,
Dublin 6, D06 HD27, Ireland.
Tel: +353 1 4923333; Fax: +353 1 4922777
E-mail: books@obrien.ie.
Website: www.obrien.ie
The O'Brien Press is a member of Publishing Ireland.

Text & photographs © contributors & School of Culinary Arts and Food Technology, 2016
Copyright for typesetting, layout, editing, design
© The O'Brien Press Ltd
Cover photography: A Fox in the Kitchen

ISBN: 978-1-84717-868-8

1 3 5 7 8 6 4 2
16 18 19 17

Printed and bound in the Czech Republic by Finidr Ltd.
The paper in this book is produced using pulp from managed forests.

Dedication

To all the staff, students, supporters and management (past and present) of the School of Culinary Arts and Food Technology, Cathal Brugha Street, who have worked with dedication over the last seventy-five years to bring about the growth of culinary education and food studies in Ireland.

Acknowledgements

If we were to mention everyone who helped in the compilation of this book, then another would be required to include them all. So please accept the school's warm thanks to all who contibuted, with our apologies to anyone we may have inadvertently omitted. The school would, however, like to express our thanks in particular to:

The incredibly hard-working team at The O'Brien Press Ltd for their support in the development of this book, especially Susan Houlden, Michael O'Brien and Emma Byrne; the hard-working contributors for their unique skills and knowledge which they expertly demonstrate in this book; the industry and trade associations, Government and public service bodies whose collective work with the School of Culinary Arts and Food Technology helps to consistently raise the standards of culinary education and food studies in Ireland; the international, national and local food and drinks companies for their research and innovation in bringing new products and services which enhance the food and beverage industry, and for their collective sponsorship of awards and scholarships which help to recognise excellence and promote creativity in the school; We thank our Innovative Supporters of Professional Industry Research, Educational and Development (INSPIRED) Friends of the Culinary Arts: Carton Bros Manor Farm Chickens, Stafford Lynch Ltd, Country Crest, Blenders, Dawn Farms, Excellence Ltd, and Musgrave MarketPlace for their continued support of the School of Culinary Arts and Food Technology.

Recipe and Photograph Credits

The school and publishers would like to thank the following photographers, videographers, individuals, current and former colleagues for permission to reproduce illustrative material in this book: food photographer and DIT culinary lecturer Dermot Seberry; Ronan Seberry and Foodeducators.ie for food photography; David Matthews and Foodeducators.ie for QR codes; Fox in the Kitchen for front cover photography, and photographs on pp74-5. The school would also like to thank the following companies for permission to reproduce copyright illustrative material: Carlow Brewing Company Ltd (pp198, 199 top) and Bitburger Braugruppe GmbH (p199).

Please consume alcohol responsibly; never drink and drive. See alcoholireland.ie/facts.

Contents

Mains

Desserts

Breads & Baking

Cocktails

The Tax Collector *Trudy Matthews*

Valley of Fire *Frank Cullen*

B-52

Hot Shot

Alcohol-free Cocktails

Elderflower & Mint Lemonade

Mint Tea Mischief *Daniel Tinsley*

Nickie Noggy Noo *Nickie Connolly*

Virgin Mule

Entertaining

The Future of Food

Management and Members of the School of Culinary Arts and Food Technology (formerly the School of Hotel and Catering Operations), 1991 (**above**) and 2016 (**below**).

Who's Who?

DARINA ALLEN

Darina is an award-winning Irish chef, food writer, TV personality and founder of Ballymaloe Cookery School in Shanagarry, County Cork. She is a graduate of Cathal Brugha Street and is a leader of the Slow Food movement in Ireland and instrumental in establishing farmers markets in Ireland. She is a member of many culinary associations and her book *30 Years at Ballymaloe* was winner of an Irish Book Award (The Avonmore Cookbook of the Year award).

DR RÓISÍN BURKE

Róisín developed molecular gastronomy as a subject discipline in the School of Culinary Arts and Food Technology, and led the development of the programme BSc (Hons) in Culinary Science. Róisín co-ordinates the Erasmus Mundus Food Innovation Product Design programme and is published widely in journals, giving lectures in Ireland and abroad.

THERESE CADDEN

Therese is a lecturer in culinary science and food product development in the School of Culinary Arts and Food Technology. Prior to this she spent ten years working in the food industry in the chilled and frozen food-processing sector and the beverage sector.

JAMES CARBERRY

James is a lecturer in the School of Culinary Arts and Food Technology, specialising in culinary arts and professional cookery. He has worked at the highest level within the hotel and catering sector, including the Michelin-three-star restaurant Georges Blanc, Vonnas, France, and is a recipient of the prestigious Roux Scholarship (for Elite Chefs).

DR KAREN CASEY

Karen lectures in nutrition, health promotion and physiology in Cathal Brugha Street. She has a PhD from King's College London, is published in journals and is a member of various nutrition bodies. She has a keen interest in sports nutrition and has worked with athletes, in particular award-winning GAA football teams.

DIARMUID CAWLEY

Diarmuid lectures in Wine Studies and Professional Cookery at the School of Culinary Arts and Food Technology, with over twenty years of national and international experience as a chef and sommelier. A David Gumbleton Memorial Award Winner in culinary arts and silver medallist in Best Sommelier in Ireland 2012, his current PhD research is in political food policy.

JOHN CLANCY

John started teaching Culinary Arts at Cathal Brugha Street in 1985. An award-winning chef with eight honorary memberships who has worked in top Dublin hotels (Russell Hotel, Jury's Hotel), he is a past president (Panel of Chefs of Ireland) and a former chief expert (World Skills Competitions). John is current Director of Education for World Chefs, with responsibility for developing certification and global standards of education and training for chefs in over 100 countries.

DERRY CLARKE

Derry has been Chef/Patron of l'Ecrivain for over twenty-six years. His restaurant has received many accolades, such as Best Restaurant and Best Chef Awards since 1999 and a Michelin Star since 2003. He has supported past and present students. An author of two successful cookbooks, *Not Just a Cookbook* and *Keeping it Simple*, he is committed to the very best local, fresh produce cooked with flair and imagination.

ABIGAIL COLLERAN

Abigail is a graduate of Cathal Brugha Street. With another graduate, Charlene O'Dowd, she co-owns and operates a custom bakery business in Galway, called 'Sugar and Spice Pantry'. They bake for both wholesale and private clients using the finest quality ingredients to produce fabulous cakes and bakes.

DENISE CONNAUGHTON

Denise has been lecturing on the Baking and Pastry Arts programme in Cathal Brugha Street for eighteen years. Prior to this, she worked in small and medium-sized craft bakeries (including Odlum's Mills and Jacob's Biscuits as a process analyst and product developer). She also holds a master's degree in third-level learning and teaching.

MARGARET CONNOLLY

A graduate turned lecturer at Cathal Brugha Street since 2000, Margaret's current doctoral research is exploring consumer wine choices in the restaurant environment.

She is a recipient of the International Savoy Educational Trust award for academic excellence and has successfully competed in Irish Guild of Sommeliers competitions. Her career in the food service industry spans three decades of work in Ireland, Germany and Australia.

RICHARD CORRIGAN

Richard is Chef/Patron of Corrigan's Mayfair, Bentley's Oyster Bar and Grill and Bentley's Sea Grill in Harrods in the UK. A graduate of Cathal Brugha Street, his first Michelin star was awarded when he was Head Chef of Stephen Bull in Fulham, London, in 1994, and he has been crowned winner of the Great British Menu on three occasions. Richard holds an Honorary Doctorate from DIT for his outstanding international achievements in the culinary arts and hospitality industry.

ANNA CRUICKSHANK

Anna is a lecturer of innovative food product development and culinary science in the School of Culinary Arts and Food Technology. Prior to this, she spent fifteen years working in the food industry in the chilled and frozen food-processing sector as a food formulation specialist.

KENNETH CULHANE

Kenneth is Head Chef at The Dysart in Petersham, Surrey, England. A Roux Scholar, and graduate of Cathal Brugha Street, he has developed his own fresh and distinctive style of cooking that encompasses the very best of natural ingredients, and uses classical traditional techniques with Asian influences.

DR FRANK CULLEN

Frank is the Head of School and has published in

national and international academic journals. Having worked for fifteen years in the hospitality industry, he joined Cathal Brugha Street as a lecturer in restaurant management in 1990. Frank is a national and international award-winner in cocktail-making, napkin folding, flambé (side table cookery) and restaurant service. He leads a team of highly professional culinary educators in the School.

PAULINE DANAHER

Pauline is an educational and industry specialist in food, cookery and molecular gastronomy, and has lectured at the School since 1995. In 2010 Pauline co-produced the Gala Irish Banquet for over two hundred of the world's leading chefs, food writers, academics, scientists, and general foodies. She has participated in 'Edible at Trinity College Dublin', creating a molecular dining experience based on Irish-grown produce. Pauline has recently completed a master's in Culinary Innovation and Food Product Development.

SHANNON DICKSON

Shannon has over twenty years' experience in the food industry in Ireland, Canada and Australia and has been a lecturer on both the Bakery and Culinary Arts Programmes at Cathal Brugha Street since 2012. She continues to work in her field of expertise adapting classical dishes for the creation of contemporary bakery and confectionary products.

ANN-MARIE DUNNE

Ann-Marie is lecturer on the Bakery Programme in DIT since 1993. As a child, she began baking with her mother and progressed to baking at a small craft bakery; she carried out her formal baking studies at The National Bakery School in Dublin and has worked and trained across Europe for many years.

PETER EVERETT

Peter is a Culinary Arts graduate of Cathal Brugha Street and a Eurotoques Young Chef of the Year winner (2007). He is Sous Chef to Graham Neville at Restaurant FortyOne on St Stephen's Green in Dublin. He has a passion for the excellent quality of Irish produce.

DR KATHLEEN FARRELL

Kathleen is a lecturer in food entrepreneurship and management in Cathal Brugha Street. Having worked in the hospitality industry for many years, she contributes to both national and international conferences. She is a member of the American Academy of Management and the Women in Business Network, an initiative of the Local Enterprise Office, Dublin.

MARK FARRELL

Mark is an award-winning culinary arts tutor, Secretary of The Panel of Chefs of Ireland, Leinster Branch and a Graduate of Hautes Études du Goût. His academic interests include developing fully inclusive culinary arts programmes using assistive technology, with an emphasis on student creativity and innovation.

SHEONA FOLEY

Sheona is a member of the Culinary Arts academic staff at DIT. Prior to this she worked in the bakery sector as a food product developer and bakery technologist. She also ran her own private catering business, servicing the private and corporate sector. Her current research interest revolves around issues of sustainability in the food industry.

JAMES FOX

A former graduate of Cathal Brugha Street, James is a lecturer in the School of Culinary Arts and Food Technology, with many years' experience in diverse cuisines and cooking techniques in Dublin's best restaurants and abroad.

CATHERINE FULVIO

Catherine is a TV chef, food writer and owner of Ballyknocken House and Cookery School in County Wicklow. She is passionate about simple yet delicious recipes, using seasonal, locally sourced ingredients wherever possible. Catherine works closely with lecturers and students of Cathal Brugha Street presenting special culinary demonstration classes.

CONRAD GALLAGHER

Conrad is an award-winning chef/restaurateur, television personality and author. He has worked with Cathal Brugha Street throughout his career. He has cooked for President Bill Clinton and guests at the White House, and his restaurant Peacock Alley, Dublin was awarded a Michelin star between 1998 and 2002. He spends his time travelling and sharing his expertise around the world.

ROSE GREENE

Rose is a graduate of Cathal Brugha Street who focuses on the importance of sustainability, reduction of food waste and use of organic and local produce. She has worked in several countries. In 2015 she opened a new restaurant, De Superette, in Gent, Belgium.

JAMES GRIFFIN

James lectures part-time in Bakery and Pastry Arts at Cathal Brugha Street. He is a sixth-generation owner and the Managing Director of Griffin's Bakery, in Galway, a former president of Richemont Club Ireland, and a regular international jury member of Louis Lesaffre Cup and Coupe Du Monde de la Boulangerie (one of the world's most prestigious bakery contests).

DARREN HARRIS

Darren is lecturer in Bakery and Pastry Arts at Cathal Brugha Street, specialising in bakery technology, functional foods and product development.

KEELAN HIGGS

Keelan is a graduate of Culinary Arts from DIT Cathal Brugha Street. He has worked in Dublin restaurants, including the Michelin two-star Restaurant Guilbaud, Chapter One, the Greenhouse, and the former Locks Brasserie. In September 2015 Keelan and Conor O'Dowd opened Locks 1 Windsor Terrace, Dublin, serving modern Irish cuisine with an emphasis on seasonal produce, great music and cocktails.

SEAN HOGAN

Sean is a lecturer in Restaurant Food and Beverage Service at Cathal Brugha Street. He has worked at the highest level in fine dining and restaurant management in locations such as the Royal Hibernian Hotel, Dawson Street, and the five-star Berkeley Court Hotel, Dublin. Sean has also served as international judge in Advanced Food Service Skills in Hotel Olympia for the Department of Education Science.

ROBERT HUMPHRIES

Robert has been a lecturer of DIT bakery and pastry arts programmes for over thirty years. A graduate of the National Bakery School in Bakery Production and Management, he worked in the industry for ten years before joining the DIT Bakery School, Kevin Street, now Cathal Brugha Street. A past president of the Institute of Irish Bakers, he has won many national and international awards.

NORMA KELLY

Norma studied Culinary Arts at Dublin Institute of Technology and worked as a pastry chef both in Dublin and abroad. She joined the teaching team at Cathal Brugha Street, and teaches pastry. Norma has a keen interest in national and international competitions, such as the World Chocolate Masters.

PAUL KELLY

Paul is a lecturer with Cathal Brugha Sreet, helping to develop new pastry and baking programmes. He is Executive Pastry Chef at The Merrion Hotel, Dublin and has won many medals in international competitions. He judges on *The Great Irish Bake Off* TV Show and is an international judge for the World Association of Chefs.

RUTH LAPPIN

A graduate of Cathal Brugha Street and winner of Euro-Toques Young Chef of the Year, 2015, Ruth is a rising culinary star and works as a chef de partie in Restaurant Patrick Guilbaud, Dublin.

ROSS LEWIS

Ross is an award-winning Irish Michelin star head chef, co-owner of the restaurant Chapter One, author and former commissioner general of Eurotoques. He studied dairy science at University College Cork and perfected his chef's knowledge and skills working in locations like Odin's, owned by Peter Langan, and the Beau Rivage Hotel in Switzerland. He opened Chapter One in 1992 and has worked closely with Cathal Brugha Street for over twenty-five years.

DR MÁIRTÍN MAC CON IOMAIRE

Máirtín is an award-winning chef, food historian, lecturer, broadcaster and ballad singer. He completed his PhD in 2009 on the History of Dublin Restaurants. He has published widely in peer-reviews and trade journals. He is the co-founder and chair of the Dublin Gastronomy Symposium and he is co-editor of *Tickling the Palate: Gastronomy in Irish Literature and Culture*. He is a trustee of the Oxford Symposium on Food and Cookery, and is a regular contributor to the media.

NEVEN MAGUIRE

Neven is an award-winning chef, owner of MacNean House & Restaurant and Cookery School in Blacklion, County Cavan, and has his own TV series, *Home Chef.* He has worked in the world's top restaurants, including Arzak, San Sebastian, Spain (3 Michelin stars) and Restaurant Léa Linster, Luxembourg (2 Michelin stars). Neven has worked with the School of Culinary Arts and Food Technology for many years.

STEPHEN MCALLISTER

Stephen started his first chef's job in Chez Hugo. He has worked in many of the top Dublin restaurants, including The Commons, which achieved one Michelin Star during his tenure. He is Head Chef on the popular TV show *The Restaurant*, and in 2008, he opened The Pig's Ear Restaurant, Nassau Street, Dublin, creating a unique Irish dining experience in a relaxed environment. Stephen has worked closely with Cathal Brugha Street for many years.

JAMES MCCAULEY

Jim worked in the Irish food industry for over ten years in sales and marketing roles. He lectures at Cathal Brugha Street in Services Marketing and Retail Food Marketing. He has recently developed a new programme in the School, the Higher Certificate in Food Sales and Culinary Practice.

MARTIN MEADE

Martin is a third generation hospitality graduate of DIT Cathal Brugha Street and winner of many National and International hospitality awards. His career spans over twenty-five years in the industry and he has worked and trained in some of the most prestigious restaurants and hotels in Ireland and abroad. Martin is currently the General Manager of Bijou Bistro in Rathgar.

MARK MORIARTY

Mark holds a BA Culinary Arts degree from Cathal Brugha Street, and is winner of the prestigious S. Pellegrino Young Chef for 2015. He embraces his Irishness in his dishes and has worked in some top restaurants in Ireland and abroad, including The Ledbury, London, Thornton's and The Greenhouse, Dublin. Mark runs his own business, The Culinary Counter (a monthly pop-up dining experience).

DIARMAID MURPHY

Diarmaid is a member of the academic staff of Cathal Brugha Street and holds a master's degree in Culinary Innovation and Food Product Development. He has also worked as a chef and executive head chef in many world-renowned restaurants and hotels, specialising in fine dining. Diarmaid has a keen interest in traditional foods and modernist cuisine.

DIARMUID MURPHY

Diarmuid lectures in Culinary Arts at the school, specialising in the study of gastronomy and food studies, with a particular emphasis on the history/culture and sociology of food and the industry in general. Prior to this, he was a chef for thirty-six years and was trained in classical French Cuisine mostly in London, France and Ireland. Currently he is undertaking his PhD studies within the institute.

JAMES MURPHY

James is a lecturer in bar and beverage studies at Cathal Brugha Street, and winner of many national and international awards, including World Champion for Elite Bartenders, 1993. A former education chairman of the International Bartenders' Association (IBA) and past president of the Bartenders' Association of Ireland (BAI), he serves as external examiner and educational advisor to many trade associations and colleges. He is the author of many bar, beverage management and responsible service publications, including *Responsible Sales and Service of Alcohol for Tourism, Hospitality and Retail Industries*.

MICHAEL O'MEARA

Michael has worked as a professional chef for almost thirty years. He is Chef and Proprietor of Oscar's Seafood Bistro in Galway city. He holds a master's degree in Culinary Innovation and Food Product Development from Cathal Brugha Street and is the author of *Sea Gastronomy: Fish and Shellfish of the North Atlantic*.

BRONA RAFTERY

Brona has been a lecturer in Culinary Arts with the School for ten years. Prior to this, she ran her own business. She has a keen interest in nutrition, healthy eating and developing recipes and menus for restricted diets and is involved in the development of artisan courses.

MICHEL ROUX SNR

Michel is truly inspirational, one of the world's most respected chefs, holding the coveted three Michelin stars consistently for more than thirty years at the Waterside Inn, West Berkshire, England. He is a prolific author of many best-selling cookery books and, with his brother Albert, the founder of the prestigious Roux Scholarship, which has been won by James Carberry and Kenneth Culhane of Cathal Brugha Street. The School is truly honoured to have Michel's recipes featured in this book.

DERMOT SEBERRY

Dermot is a lecturer in Culinary Arts at Cathal Brugha Street. He worked world-wide as a professional chef for sixteen years. He is an author of four published books, one of which, *Ireland – A Culinary Journey in the North East*, was nominated 'Best in World' by the Gourmand World Cookbook Awards. His FoodTour.ie event draws international foodies to Ireland's Ancient East from over twenty-five different countries each year. Food photography is another of Dermot's passions.

JAMES SHERIDAN

James is a lecturer in food and beverage studies and restaurant management at Cathal Brugha Street, with twelve years' industry experience across many establishments, including The Shelbourne Hotel and L'Ecrivain Restaurant. Awarded a medallion of excellence at the World Skills Competition in 2007, he has a master's degree in Hospitality Management and is pursuing a PhD in the area of consumer behaviour.

GEORGE SMITH

George is a lecturer in Culinary Arts at Cathal Brugha Street and a winner of the prestigious Jean Conail World Master Chef Trophy, in 1998. Former captain of the Irish Senior Culinary Team and World Skills expert in cookery for the Department of Education and Science, he coaches the Irish Junior Culinary Team.

KEVIN THORNTON

Kevin is a graduate and former lecturer in professional cookery at Cathal Brugha Street. He is also an Irish celebrity chef and author of *Food for Life*. Owner of the award-winning Thornton's Restaurant in Dublin's city centre, he was the first Irish chef to achieve two Michelin stars. Kevin has received numerous awards, including Chef of the Year for Ireland, and has been described as a 'gastronomic legend' in Ireland.

Nurturing Excellence

On Bloomsday, 16 June 1941, the doors of what became Cathal Brugha Street opened, beginning a long tradition of nurturing excellence in generations of Irish students in all aspects of food, beverage and hospitality.

This book celebrates the development of what is now known as the School of Culinary Arts and Food Technology (SCAFT) from its origins in 1941 to the present day and showcases how it has been at the heart of training and educating chefs, waiters, restaurateurs, and hotel and catering staff for decades, and in more recent years, butchers, bar managers and bakers.

Established as Saint Mary's College of Domestic Science, under the auspices of the City of Dublin Vocational Education Committee (CDVEC), the focus and name of the college changed in the early 1950s to the Dublin College of Catering to address the training needs of the burgeoning Irish tourism industry.

The courses offered in 1941 were household management, institutional management, hotel cookery (girls), apprentice chefs (boys), tearoom cookery, nutrition and dietetics, and a diploma course for the training of teachers. The first principal of the new college was Kathleen O'Sullivan (1941–1950), and she was succeeded by Winifred Boucher-Hayes (1951–1969) and Gertie Armstrong (1969–1973). Teaching staff included Josephine Marnell, Nora Breathnach, Anne Martin and Mor Murnaghan, the compilers of *All in the Cooking,* a hugely popular textbook from 1946 to well into the 1970s. So popular indeed was their book that it was successfully re-issued in 2015.

In 1941, with the opening of Cathal Brugha Street, chefs' and waiters' courses transferred from Parnell Square where they had begun in 1927. Bill Ryan and Liam Kavanagh were among the first students to attend and recall that the chefs (boys) had to use the side stairs of the building for fear they would see up the girls' skirts on the front stairs! Both Bill and Liam travelled extensively around the world, working on luxury Cunard cruise ships. Liam spent five years in New York City in the 1950s, and Bill trained a young Colin O'Daly (The Park, Roly's Bistro) in the restaurant at Dublin Airport, which at the time was one of Ireland's best restaurants. In Cathal Brugha

Top: Principal of the college, Winifred Boucher-Hayes (1951–1969). **Bottom:** Mor Murnaghan, a former teacher and one of the compilers of the popular textbook *All in the Cooking.*

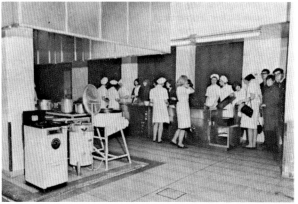

Above left: Bill Ryan and Liam Kavanagh at the Savoy Hotel, London, 1948.

Above middle: School kitchen in the 1940s.

Above right: The brochure celebrating twenty-five years of the College of Catering, Cathal Brugha Street, 1941–1966.

Street, young apprentices were trained by a Swiss chef, Johnny Annler and a French chef, Beaucaire Murphy.

In this post-war period a fledgling tourist industry was emerging in need of professionally trained hospitality staff. By 1954 a three-year hotel management certificate course was available. Chefs Annler and Murphy were succeeded by Irish chefs PJ Dunne, of Jammet's, and Michael Ganly (*c*1958). Many graduates remember the militaristic focus Ganly had on clean, ironed uniforms and the importance of being clean shaven. Ken Switzer, a chef graduate, recalled 'the training you receive in Cathal Brugha Street is so professional and so thorough that you really can travel anywhere with it.' PJ Dunne was the larder chef and regaled his students with stories of how he used monkfish tails to fashion scampi, lobster and scallop dishes in Jammet's during the shortage years of the Second World War.

DIPLOMAS

In the 1960s Jimmy Kilbride, who had trained under Karl Uhlemann in the Gresham Hotel and then became chef at Dublin Airport, joined the teaching staff bringing a new dynamism with him. In the early part

Below left: PJ Dunne with students in 1978. . **Below right:** Jimmy Kilbride and George Smith.

of this decade the certificate course was converted to a three-year diploma course with the first graduates emerging in 1965.

By 1968 there was a range of full-time courses in areas such as hotel reception, accommodation management, and apprentice waiters. Part-time courses were available for working chefs and waiters. Kevin O'Rourke was teaching restaurant service in Cathal Brugha Street at this time.

In 1968, Darina Allen (née O'Connell) graduated from Cathal Brugha Street, and found that most restaurants at that time would not have women in their kitchens. Mor Murnaghan introduced her to Myrtle Allen, in Ballymaloe House, starting a life-long partnership, with Darina marrying Myrtle's son Tim. Myrtle was awarded an Honorary PhD from DIT in 2014, and there has been a long relationship between Ballymaloe and DIT with the

placement of students and the employment of graduates.

MOVES TOWARDS DEGREE STATUS

In 1971 the work of the college was divided into three departments which later (in 1982) evolved into schools of their own: Hotel and Catering Administration, Hotel and Catering Operations, and Home and Social Sciences. The Department of Hotel and Catering Operations, under the leadership of Joseph Hegarty, provided service teaching to the other departments and was subsequently renamed the School of Culinary Arts and Food Technology (SCAFT).

In 1973 a four-year Higher Diploma in Hotel and Catering Management course commenced, and it was granted degree status by Dublin University in 1977. In 1977 City & Guilds advanced master

chef courses in both kitchen and larder, and in pastry were being taught by Jimmy Kilbride and John Linnane. Their students became teachers, entrepreneurs and leaders in the culinary, hospitality and restaurant industry in the last decades of the twentieth century. Some of these, including Joe Erraught, Noel Cullen, Pierce Hingston and Eugene McGovern represented Ireland on the National Culinary Team at Hotelympia in London and at other international culinary competitions with great success. Kilbride engendered a love of learning and instilled confidence in Irish chefs, asserting that they were world-class.

One such graduate, Kevin Thornton, became the first Irish chef to be awarded two Michelin stars in 2001. Thornton recalls that the only person he was ever nervous cooking for after opening his own restaurant was Jimmy Kilbride, 'It was like cooking for the master.' At the age of sixty, Kilbride retired to open his own business, Kilbride Cuisine, which is still very successful and run by his son.

Kilbride's shoes were filled by Jim Bowe who inspired the next generation of Irish chefs, including many of the current culinary lecturers in DIT (and contributors to this book), for example James Carberry, who won the Roux Scholarship in 1992. Another of his protégés was Richard Corrigan, now a celebrated television chef and restaurateur, who Bowe recalls arrived in on his motorbike from Meath ahead of his class mates every morning hail, rain or snow.

FROM CERT TO DEGREES

In the 1980s the full-time student body grew from 500 to over 1,000. Part-time programmes, particularly in professional cookery, increased, along with full-time courses that were funded by CERT (the Council for Education, Recruitment and Training, established in 1963). In 1977, courses were streamlined, new services were funded by the EEC, and in 1982 the new National Craft Curriculum Certification Board (NCCCB) enabled catering education in Ireland to set its own standards and award its own certificates.

In 1986 a full-time certificate in culinary arts was developed with a focus on catering for health. This was to supply diet cooks to the hospitals, including the newly opened private hospitals of the Blackrock Clinic and the Mater Private. Many graduates also went on to work in the wider hospitality industry and to further their studies. Clare Gilsenan, for example, joined the BA (Hons) Culinary Arts in DIT in 1999 and went on to earn her PhD in 2010 and is currently a lecturer in Galway-Mayo Institute of Technology (GMIT).

In 1999, the new primary degree in Culinary Arts became the first degree programme in the world to have cooking as a core module through all four years. The first cohort graduated in 2003. Quite a number of the graduates from this programme have contributed to this book, and even more of them are currently holding management positions in the leading hotels and restaurants, both in Ireland and internationally. Kenneth Culhane, for example, won the Roux Scholarship in 2010; Rose Greene won the UK Young Chef of the Year in 2009; and many of the winners of the annual Euro-toques Young Irish Chef competition over recent years have come from this programme – Abigail Colleran, Peter Everett, Ciarán Elliot, Mark Moriarty and Ruth Lappin – or the Professional Cookery Certificate programme – Christine Cullen, Peter Byrne and Ian Ussher.

Above left: DIT lecturer John Clancy in action.

Above middle: Eugene Kane, DIT lecturer, and student Derek Blake, in the Bakery School, 1989.

Above right (left to right): Therese O'Sullivan, Miriam Chadwick and Orla Murphy preparing for a presidential visit in the then-new Kevin Street Bakery School, 1991.

SCHOOL EXPANDS TO INCLUDE BAKERY, MEAT TECHNOLOGY AND BAR

In 2002, all food-related programmes in DIT were brought together under the School of Culinary Arts and Food Technology. They were the Department of Bar and Meat Technology, Department of Baking Technology (The National Bakery School) and a Department of the Culinary Arts (previously known as the Department of Hotel and Catering Operations). The National Bakery School (founded in 1937)

remained based in Kevin Street until 2010 when two new bakery kitchens were built in Cathal Brugha Street. The Department of Bar and Meat Management had been under the School of Commerce and Retail Distribution in the College of Art and Design, Mountjoy Square. In 2010, both departments were relocated to Cathal Brugha Street.

Additional courses were developed in SCAFT during Aodán Ó Cearbhail's term as Head of School, including a master's degree in Culinary Innovation

Below left: DIT lecturer Pat Zaiden teaching butchery techniques.

Below middle: Internal competitions hone skills in cocktail-making.

Below right: Gresham Hotel head bartender Jerry Fitzpatrick demonstrating at Cathal Brugha Street.

and Food Product Development, chaired by Anna Cruickshank (2006); a four-year BSc (Honours) in Bar Studies (Management & Entrepreneurship); a four-year BSc (Honours) in Culinary Entrepreneurship; and a three-year BSc (Ordinary) in Baking & Pastry Arts Management, all chaired by Head of School Frank Cullen and launched in 2006.

FROM STRENGTH TO STRENGTH – GRADUATE SUCCESS IN 2015

The School continued to win accolades in 2015. In July, Mark Moriarty was crowned the S. Pellegrino Young Chef 2015 in Milan, beating nineteen other regional finalists from all over the world. In November, Ruth Lappin was crowned Euro-toques Irish Young Chef of the Year 2015, and won a stage working with Clare Smyth MBE in Restaurant Gordon Ramsay in London. At the end of the year, when Catherine Cleary of *The Irish Times* handed out her food 'Oscars', over half of the winning establishments employed Cathal Brugha Street graduates, and nearly half of

the chef/proprietor winners were DIT graduates. The overall award for best dinner 2015 was for 'Mews' in Baltimore, set up by Luke Matthews and Robert Collender (both 2008 Graduates), and the runner-up was 'Bastible' in Leonards Corner, where Bill Ó Cléirigh (2014 Culinary Arts graduate) was running the front of house. The future does indeed look bright.

This book combines a selection of recipes, tips and views from our lecturers in the culinary, bar, bakery, wine, product development, gastronomy and entrepreneurship areas of the School. It also includes contributions from graduates such as Darina Allen, Kevin Thornton, Michael O'Meara, Abigail Colleran, Rose Greene and James Griffin. The School is also proud to include contributions from broader industry partners and chefs including Derry Clarke, Catherine Fulvio, Neven Maguire, Ross Lewis and Michel Roux Snr, who all have a strong relationship with Cathal Brugha Street as mentors and employers of our students and graduates.

The Cathal Brugha kitchens, 2015.

Award-winners

Above (left to right): Mark Moriarty, S. Pellegrino, Best Young Chef, 2015; Robert Humphries, Bakery World Cup 2006; George Smith, Master Chef World Champion, 1998; **Below (left to right):** James Murphy, Martini Grand Prix World Champion, 1993; Shane Fitzpatrick, General Manager of Radisson Blu, Cork, pictured here as silver medallist, World Skills Restaurant Service.

STARTERS

CATHERINE FULVIO

Artichoke, Roast Parsnip & Walnut Salad

'For the last few years, artichokes have flourished in my garden. We have so many that I even use the gorgeous purple flowers for arrangements to bring more of the outdoors indoors.' *Catherine Fulvio*

Serves 4

For the Salad:
Extra virgin olive oil
4-5 parsnips, sliced into thin wedges
Rocket or any favourite garden leaves
12 artichoke hearts, cut into wedges
12 cherry tomatoes, washed and halved
100g walnuts, lightly toasted and roughly chopped
Rosemary croutons, to garnish (*see below*)

For the Dressing:
2 tbsp walnut oil
1 tbsp sunflower oil
1 tbsp white wine vinegar
1½ tsp wholegrain mustard
Salt and freshly ground black pepper

1 Preheat the oven to 180°C.
2 Combine all the ingredients for the dressing in a jar with a lid and shake to combine. Season to taste.
3 Drizzle a roasting pan with olive oil, toss the parsnips in and roast for about 20 minutes, until crisp and golden.
4 Arrange the rocket or other garden leaves on a serving platter.
5 Mix the artichoke wedges, cherry tomatoes and walnuts with a little dressing in a bowl.
6 Arrange the parsnips around the edge of the leaves. Spoon the artichokes, cherry tomatoes and walnuts onto the rocket.
7 Drizzle with a little more dressing and garnish with rosemary croutons.

Chef's Tip
To keep things local, make rosemary croutons by dicing 3 slices of Irish soda bread. Mix 2 tbsp olive oil and 2 tsp chopped rosemary, a little salt and freshly ground black pepper in a large bowl and toss the diced bread in the rosemary oil. Place onto a roasting pan and bake in the oven at 180°C for about 15-20 minutes, keeping an eye on them and turning them from time to time.

Drinks
A Northern Rhone Syrah or wheat beer.

ARTICHOKE, ROAST PARSNIP & WALNUT SALAD **29**

CONRAD GALLAGHER

Pumpkin Risotto with
Trompettes de Mort & Pancetta

'An ideal dish to serve at Thanksgiving or Hallowe'en when pumpkins are in season.'
Conrad Gallagher

Serves 4

For the Risotto

2 tbsp butter

2 shallots, finely diced

1 clove garlic, crushed

1 tsp thyme

250g (1¼ cups) Arborio rice

250ml (1 cup) white wine

Approx. 950ml (1 quart) hot
  vegetable stock

125ml (½ cup) heavy cream

100g (1 cup) grated Parmesan

60g (about ¾ cup) pancetta, thinly
  sliced

115g *trompettes de mort* (black
  chanterelles), sautéed in 60g (½
  stick/¼ cup) butter

85g (¼ cup) mascarpone

1 tbsp diced red pepper for
  garnishing

For the Pumpkin Purée

2 small pumpkins, peeled, seeded
  and diced

2 cloves garlic, crushed

60ml (¼ cup) olive oil

3 sprigs thyme

FOR THE PUREÉ:

1 Preheat the oven to 200°C. Place the pumpkin in a heavy,
   ovenproof pan with the garlic, olive oil and thyme. Roast
   for 30 minutes, remove from the oven and let cool.

2 Transfer to a food processor, blend until smooth, push
   through a fine sieve into a bowl. Rinse out the pan.

FOR THE RISOTTO:

1 Melt the butter in the pan. Add the shallots, garlic and
   thyme, cover and sweat over medium heat until soft.
   Add the rice and white wine.

2 Cover and sweat for about 2 minutes on a medium
   heat, then uncover and let reduce until almost dry.

3 Gradually add the vegetable stock to the rice, stirring
   continuously after each addition until all the stock has
   been absorbed and the rice is tender.

4 Mix the cream and the Parmesan into the risotto, mix in
   the pumpkin purée.

TO SERVE

Serve in bowls, with the pancetta and *trompettes de mort*
on top. Add a spoonful of mascarpone and garnish with
diced pepper.

Drinks

Sauvignon Blanc (California), Frascati or Pilsner lager.

JAMES FOX

Crab Claws with Garlic, Caper Berries & Parsley Cream

'Traditionally Irish brown crab was sold as a whole live product. However, excellent quality crab and claw meat and fresh crab claws are now readily available which makes crab much more accessible to home cooks and gourmets. This dish is extremely flavourful.' *James Fox*

Serves 4

24 Irish crab claws
120ml cream
50g butter, softened
2 cloves garlic, finely minced
15g flat leaf parsley, finely chopped
10g caper berries
4 lemon wedges

1 Mix the softened butter with the garlic. Set aside.
2 Heat a frying pan over a medium heat. Add the cream and crab claws. Simmer for approximately 2 minutes until the claws are heated through.
3 Allow the garlic butter to gently melt into the cream and lower the heat (do not allow to boil).
4 Add in the caper berries and chopped parsley.

TO SERVE:
Drizzle the crab claws with the cream sauce, garnish with a wedge of lemon, and serve with green salad and grilled ciabatta.

Drinks
German Riesling wine, ideally dry to off-dry or a Pilsner lager.

DERMOT SEBERRY

Crispy Hen's Egg with Black Pudding & Pea Purée

'A classically elegant dish, the flavours marry beautifully, and the ingredients display especially well when served on a white plate.' Dermot Seberry

Serves 4

4 free-range hen eggs at room
   temperature
1 tsp salt
1 tbsp white vinegar
4 slices of Clonakilty black pudding
4 slices of smoked streaky bacon
150g frozen peas
4 tsp fresh mint, chopped
1 knob of butter
1 pinch of bread soda
200ml vegetable oil

For the Crumb Coating:
3 free-range eggs, beaten
150ml milk
Small bowl all-purpose flour
200g Panko breadcrumbs

1 Place eggs into a small pot of boiling salted water with the vinegar (to help release the shell), simmer 5 minutes and chill in a bowl of iced water for 10 minutes.
2 Combine the beaten egg and milk. Remove shells and coat each egg in flour. Dip the floured eggs into the beaten egg and coat in the crumbs. Set aside.
3 For the pea purée: cook peas and mint in boiling water, with salt and bread soda (to keep the green colour) for 4 minutes. Strain and save the liquid.
4 Blend peas to a fine smooth purée, add some reserved water to loosen the purée if necessary. If the purée is grainy, pass it through a sieve.
5 Grill the bacon till just crispy. Meanwhile, pan-fry the pudding till soft and warm in the centre.

TO SERVE:
1 This dish is best served freshly made. Deep-fry the coated eggs for 60 seconds in 200ml vegetable oil.
2 To create pea purée lines, spoon a large dollop of purée on one end of the plate. Drag a small spatula through the purée from one end of the plate to the other.
3 Place the pudding in the middle of the plate, and with a spoon push an indent in the centre for the egg. Top with the crispy bacon slice.

Drinks
Champagne or a dry, unoaked Chardonnay wine.

JAMES FOX

Confit of Salmon with Sauce Vierge

'Confit of Salmon can be served as a starter or as a light main course with the addition of a warm potato salad. An extremely healthy dish which accentuates the natural appearance and flavour of salmon. All elements can be prepared in advance except for the soft herbs, which should be added to the sauce vierge at the last minute.'
James Fox

Serves 4

350g skinned salmon fillet
100ml grapeseed oil
80ml olive oil
½ tbsp freshly ground coriander
 seeds
½ tsp ground white pepper
10 whole basil leaves
3 sprigs thyme and salt
½ tsp garlic, finely chopped
25g carrot and celery, chopped
3 tbsp chives, chopped
2 tbsp salmon roe, for
 presentation

For the Sauce Vierge:

2 tbsp confit oil from salmon or
 good olive oil
½ tsp ground cumin
½ tsp ground coriander
3 sprigs saffron, steeped in a
 little hot water
1 red pepper, roasted and finely
 chopped
1 tomato, finely chopped
Fresh coriander and chives,
 chopped

1 Cut the salmon fillet into neat 75g portions. Place the grapeseed oil, olive oil, coriander, pepper, basil leaves, thyme and garlic into a shallow dish. Immerse the salmon in the mixture, cover and marinate for a couple of hours.

2 To cook the fish, preheat the oven to 90°C. Place the vegetables in the tray with the salmon on top, ensuring it does not touch the tray. Cover with the marinade.

3 Cook the salmon for 10-12 minutes. The fish should remain a bright orange-red and be lukewarm.

4 Remove the fish from the marinade and allow to cool to room temperature. Strain the oil and reserve.

TO SERVE:
Place the salmon on a plate and use the reserved oil to make a sauce vierge.

TO MAKE THE SAUCE VIERGE:
Put all ingredients in a saucepan and heat until warm.

Drinks

Saumur or Montlouis-sur-Loire Chenin Blanc or a Pilsner-style lager, such as the German Krombacher Pils from North Rhine-Westphalia, or Jack Cody's Irish Puck Pilsner from Drogheda.

Dublin Bay Prawn Bisque

'This recipe represents a contemporary twist on the French classic. The shells of crustaceans not only contain valuable colour pigments which contribute to the quality of a bisque but also considerable flavour notes.' *Mark Farrell*

Serves 4

Glug of sunflower oil

500g raw prawn shells including
  heads

1 small onion, 1 carrot, 1 stick of
  celery, diced

10ml white wine

10ml brandy

8 cherry tomatoes

500ml chicken or fish stock

1 garlic clove, chopped

Bouquet garni (green leek, bay leaf,
  thyme & parsley)

50ml cream

50ml semi-whipped cream

10ml butter

50g oatmeal

1 Place oil in a hot, thick-bottomed pan and cook the prawn shells without colouring. Move and crush shells as they are cooking. Ensure there is no liquid remaining in pan before adding onion, carrot and celery.

2 Cook on moderate heat, again avoiding colour. Add wine and brandy and remove from heat.

3 Add tomatoes, stock and bouquet garni to pan, place back on heat and simmer for 25 minutes.

4 Pass through a fine sieve into a clean pan and place back on heat.

5 To the same pan add 50ml of cream and boil rapidly for 3 minutes to reduce.

6 Remove from heat and check, correct seasoning. Pour into jug.

7 Warm the butter in a small pan and add oatmeal, cook stirring continually until the oats are evenly browned.

8 Warm some heat-resistant glasses with hot water, drain and add the hot bisque from the jug, top with semi-whipped cream and toasted oatmeal.

Variation

For a thicker soup, a roux can be used to give additional body to the soup. As an alternative to prawn shells, lobster or crayfish shells can be substituted to provide a rich and colourful menu option.

Drinks

Dry sherry, Chenin Blanc wine or a pale lager, such as Irish Cloughmore Granite lager, from the Whitewater Brewery, County Down.

Chef's Tip

Crustacean shells can also be frozen, to be cooked at a later date as required.

PAULINE DANAHER

Middle-Eastern-Inspired Fresh Vegetable Salad

'The inspiration for this salad is Middle Eastern. The combination of the fresh salad ingredients with the Middle Eastern spices would work very well as a side dish as well as a starter.' *Pauline Danaher*

Serves 4

200g cucumber

300g vine tomatoes

180g radishes

1 red pepper, deseeded

1 red onion

30g coriander leaves, roughly chopped

10g flat leaf parsley, chopped

100ml olive oil

Grated zest and juice of 1 lemon

1½ tsp sherry vinegar

1 garlic clove, crushed

1 tsp ground cardamom

1½ tsp ground allspice

1 tsp ground cumin

Salt and pepper

1 Dice the cucumber, tomato, radish, red pepper and red onion. Mix together in a bowl with the parsley and coriander.

2 In a separate bowl or sealable container mix the spices, olive oil, vinegar, garlic and the zest and juice of the lemon until well blended. Taste for seasoning.

3 When ready to serve, add the salad dressing to the fresh vegetables and serve. The salad can also be served with pitta bread and hummus for a more substantial starter or light main dish.

Drinks

Pinot Grigio from the Alto Adige or Berliner Weisse beer.

Ham Hock Terrine with Pickled Vegetables

'All terrines and charcuterie have a degree of difficulty but producing your own is worth the patience and effort. Terrines also require a period of time to set and allow flavours to develop. Prepared in advance, this dish merely requires plating for an impressive service.' *James Fox*

Serves 8-10

For the Ham Hock Terrine:

4 fresh (unsmoked) ham hocks

1 onion, peeled and halved

4 whole garlic cloves

1 carrot, peeled and halved lengthways

2 celery sticks, chopped

2-3 thyme sprigs

25g flat leaf parsley, washed dried and finely chopped

1 bay leaf

1 tsp black peppercorns

250ml dry white wine

4 gelatine leaves

TO PREPARE HAM HOCK TERRINE:

1 Soak the ham hocks in cold water for 2 hours to decrease salt content. Discard water and pat the ham hocks dry with kitchen towel.

2 Lightly grease a 1-litre terrine or loaf tin. Line with cling wrap, leaving a generous overhang to cover the terrine when assembled.

For the Spiced Pickling Vinegar:

1 tbsp allspice berries

1 tbsp cloves

5cm-piece fresh root ginger, peeled
  and sliced

1 cinnamon stick

12 whole black peppercorns

1.2 litres white wine vinegar

250g sugar

TO MAKE THE SPICED PICKLING VINEGAR:
Place all ingredients in a saucepan and heat gently to boiling point. Simmer for 1 minute, remove from the heat, cover and leave to infuse for 1 hour. Strain and use.

For the Mixed Vegetable Pickle:

1.3kg of mixed vegetables such as
  pearl onions, carrots, cauliflower,
  green beans

175g salt

1.75 litres water

2 bay leaves

750ml spiced vinegar

5g ground turmeric

TO MAKE THE MIXED VEGETABLE PICKLE:

1 Peel and trim the vegetables as necessary. Leave the onions whole, thickly slice the carrot, cut cauliflower into small florets and cut the beans into 2.5cm lengths. Place the vegetables in a large glass bowl.

2 Put the salt and water in a large pan and warm over a low heat until the salt has dissolved completely. Leave to cool, then pour enough of the brine over the vegetables to completely cover.

3 Place a plate, slightly smaller than the diameter of the bowl on top of the vegetables to keep them submerged in the brine. Leave to stand for 24 hours.

4 Tip the vegetables into a colander to drain. Rinse very well in cold water to remove excess brine. Drain again and pat dry using kitchen paper.

5 Place the bay leaves, turmeric and spiced vinegar in a saucepan and bring to the bowl slowly over a low heat. Meanwhile, pack the brined vegetables and bay leaves into hot sterilised jars. Fill the jars almost to the top with the hot vinegar mix.

6 Gently tap the jars to release any trapped air bubbles, cover and seal. Store the pickles in a cool dark place for four weeks before consuming. Use within 1 year.

Chef's Tip

If you do not have a terrine or loaf tin, the mixture can be put into small bowls or ramekins and served as potted ham. It is best to leave it for a couple of days in the fridge before eating as this will allow all flavours to marry well. Instead of serving with pickled vegetables, try a green salad with flavoured mayonnaise sauces, such as truffle mayonnaise, wholegrain mustard mayonnaise or wasabi mayonnaise.

Drinks

Gewürztraminer or Beaujolais Cru wines or a blonde lager or blonde ale such as Belgian Leffe Blonde or Affligem Blonde; or Helvick Gold, Irish Blonde Ale.

PETER EVERETT

Courgette Flower Stuffed with Wild Mushrooms & Lovage

'This dish reflects my ethos of hearty, yet refined, seasonal cooking.' *Peter Everett*

Serves 4

4 courgette flowers

400g wild mushrooms (cepes
  work well)

100g cream

2 egg yolks

20g brandy

1 shallot, finely diced

For the Sauce:

50g onion purée

50g milk

50g lovage leaves, well blanched
  and refreshed

1 Clean and slice mushrooms.

2 In two large pans sauté the mushrooms until golden. Just before finishing cooking add a knob of butter, some seasoning and the shallot. Finish with the brandy.

3 Remove half of the sautéd mushrooms, dice finely and chill.

4 Add the cream to the pan containing the remaining mushroom mixture and cook until well reduced. Place in a blender with the egg yolks and blitz until smooth. Chill this mix, then fold in the chilled chopped mushrooms and place in a piping bag.

5 Carefully stuff the courgette flowers, trying to retain the natural shape of the flower. Steam at 80°C for 8 minutes.

TO MAKE THE SAUCE

1 Place the onion purée, milk and lovage leaves with some seasoning in a blender and blitz until bright green and smooth.

2 Froth the sauce with a hand blender and spoon into a bowl. Lift the flower on top and serve.

*Peter Everett works his liquids in
  grams in this recipe.

Drinks

A robust Rioja or dark lagers and brown ales.

KEVIN THORNTON

Little Urchin's Aren

'Picked from Ireland's western sea floor, these small spiny shellfish are treated as delicacies in Spain, Greece and Italy, and exported as far away as Japan. Sea urchin roe is considered to be an aphrodisiac. What better way to spend a day than by collecting and preparing such a beautiful delicacy?' *Kevin Thornton*

Serves 4

4 sea urchins
Half a carrot, finely diced
Quarter of a celeriac, finely diced
20ml olive oil
200ml double cream
5g unsalted butter
Half a clove of garlic, peeled
Half a shallot
Freshly milled white peppercorns

Drinks
A white Burgundy wine or a pilsner lager such as Eight Degrees Barefoot Bohemian Pilsner Lager from Cork.

TO PREPARE THE SEA URCHINS:
1 Make an incision in the top and remove a third of the urchin (much like topping an egg). Keep the top to use in the sauce. With care, remove the roe from the centre with a small teaspoon and place in a bowl.
2 Strain the juice into a separate small bowl.
3 Wash the shells and heat slightly in the oven at 50°C for 2-3 minutes.

TO MAKE THE BRUNOISE OF VEGETABLES:
Lightly sauté the celeriac and carrot in a little olive oil for 2-3 minutes. Season with pepper.

TO MAKE THE SEA URCHIN CREAM:
1 Place the cream, shallot and the garlic clove half into a pot. The shallot and garlic should only scent the cream.
2 Bring to the boil and simmer to reduce by half. Pour in the sea urchin juice and bring back to the boil. Reduce by half again.
3 Remove, pass through a fine sieve, place back in the pot and fold in the butter over a low heat.

TO SERVE:
Half fill the sea urchin shells with vegetable brunoise. Place the roe on top and add the sea urchin cream. Finish by placing the other half of the shell on top.

MARGARET CONNOLLY

Nettle Soup

'Many of our parents' generation had a strong belief in the health properties of nettles. To pick the young tender leaves from February to May was thought to improve blood circulation and lower blood pressure. This recipe for nettle soup is simple to make and is deliciously healthy and surprisingly sting free.' *Margaret Connolly*

Serves 6

75g butter

1 large or 2 medium-sized leeks

225g young nettles, washed and chopped carefully to avoid stings

225g sliced potatoes

1 litre chicken stock

150ml cream

Salt and pepper

1 Melt the butter in a heavy saucepan until foaming.

2 Add the chopped leeks and nettles.

3 Cook over a gentle heat until soft but not coloured (approx. 10 minutes), and add the potatoes and stock.

4 Simmer gently for 30-35 minutes.

5 Liquidise the soup.

6 Return to the heat and season to taste.

7 Gently add the cream and ladle into warmed soup bowls.

Variation

If preferred, onions can be used instead of leeks.

Vegetable stock can be used instead of chicken.

Drinks

Sauvignon Blanc, Soave wine, Kölsch beer from Cologne or Kentucky Kölsch from Alltech.

KENNETH CULHANE

Petersham Garden Salad with White Chocolate Mayonnaise

'This dish is greatly evocative of spring perfumes; the scents of radish and English mace leaves with their vibrant flowers all thicken the air. The composition of this salad changes with the rhythm of the garden; freshness and purity of flavour is the key to this dish.' *Kenneth Culhane*

Serves 1

For the Salad:

3 asparagus spears

10 broad beans

6 minutina leaves

8 fresh radish leaves

3 sprigs of chickweed

2 leaves of wall pepper

6 salad burnet leaves

6 English mace leaves

4 rocket flowers

2 red clover flowers and leaves

2 heartsease flowers

For the White Chocolate Mayonnaise:

150g Valrhona white chocolate, melted

150g grapeseed oil

30g light extra virgin olive oil

60g lemon juice

20g lime juice

20g rice wine vinegar

3 medium to large organic
   free-range egg yolks

30g Dijon mustard

8g salt

1g xanthan gum

TO MAKE THE WHITE CHOCOLATE MAYONNAISE:

1 Whisk egg yolks, mustard, vinegar, lemon and lime juices together over gently boiling water until the core temperature reaches 120°C.

2 Warm all the oils, including the chocolate, transfer the egg mixture to blender and emulsify slowly with oils.

3 Add salt and xanthan gum. Load into a thermal siphon and charge with two NO^2 cartridges.

TO SERVE:

1 Make fine shavings with a peeler with one of the asparagus spears, blanch the other spears, cut in half.

2 Mix the fresh broad beans and shaved and blanched asparagus with olive oil and lemon juice.

3 Season and arrange the asparagus and herbs in a natural fashion on the plate.

4 Dress with olive oil and some white chocolate mayonnaise.

Drinks

Dry rosé, Sauvignon Blanc wine, pale ale or Kentucky Ale from Alltech.

RICHARD CORRIGAN

Scotch Broth

'Sometime classic favourites are simply the best. Broth is making a welcome comeback on cold winter days.' *Richard Corrigan*

Serves 4

2 lamb necks, on the bone, each
  weighing 300-400g
50g carrots, diced
50g onion, diced
50g leek, diced
50g celery, diced
50g celeriac, diced
50g turnips, diced
3 garlic cloves, sliced
40g pearl barley
1 bouquet garni
Parsley
200ml olive oil
Salt
Pepper

1 Heat the olive oil in a large, heavy-based pan over a medium heat. Sweat all the vegetables and garlic for 5-10 minutes until soft and lightly golden.
2 Add the lamb necks, followed by the pearl barley and approximately 2 litres of cold water. Bring to the boil, season with salt and pepper and add the bouquet garni.
3 Simmer the broth for 2 hours, remove from the heat. Carefully lift the necks out of the pan and flake the meat from the bone. Discard the bones and add the flaked meat back to the broth.

TO SERVE:
Reheat the broth, adjust the seasoning to taste and stir in plenty of chopped parsley.

Drinks
Chenin Blanc wine or Scotch ale.

JAMES FOX

Tian of Crab

'A crab tian epitomises what an elegant homemade starter should be. Made slightly in advance, this light, flavourful and aesthetically pleasing dish will prove popular with guests time and time again.' *James Fox*

Serves 4

Tian:

400g crab meat

2 limes, rind and juice

100ml mayonnaise

1 chilli, de-seeded and finely
   chopped

A little salt and pepper

Dressing & Herb Garnish:

4 tbsp olive oil

1½ tbsp white wine vinegar

1 large tomato, diced

20g chives, chopped

Salt and pepper

Sprigs of parsley, mint, chervil,
   rocket, coriander, to garnish,
   if desired

Croutes:

Ciabatta bread

Olive oil

Maldon sea salt

1 Squeeze the crab meat over a colander to remove the excess moisture, transfer to a large bowl with mayonnaise, lime juice, zest and chilli, mix well and refrigerate for 10 minutes.

2 Place a tian mould (scone cutter) on each plate and fill with the crab mix (seasoned to taste), pressing it down to make sure it holds together, and then carefully remove the mould. Place the herb sprigs on top of the tian.

TO PREPARE THE DRESSING:

Mix the olive oil, vinegar, diced tomato, chopped chives, salt and pepper in a bowl and drizzle this dressing around the tian. The dressing can be processed and sieved, if desired.

HERB GARNISH:

Small sprig of parsley, small sprig of mint, small sprig of chervil, rocket leaves, sprig of coriander.

CROUTES PREPARATION:

Thinly slice some ciabatta bread at an angle. Brush with olive oil and sprinkle with Maldon salt flakes. Bake at 180°C for 8-10 minutes until crisp.

Drinks

Vouvray, Riesling wine or a Belgium Tripel beer such as Westmalle Trappist Tripel or Gouden Carolus Tripel.

GEORGE SMITH

Tortellini Filled with Braised Oxtail

'This award-winning pasta dish, served with buttered leeks, wild mushrooms and tomato chutney glazed with foie gras cream and truffle oil, won the gold medal for the Irish culinary team at World Culinary Grand Prix in 2000.' *George Smith*

Serves 4

100g oxtail

200g pasta flour

2 egg yolks

60g leeks

40g wild mushrooms

2 tomatoes

30g foie gras

500ml chicken stock

200ml cream

50g butter

3 tbsp red wine vinegar

20g sugar

1 shallot

15g tomato paste

Black olives, to garnish

1 Braise oxtails in stock in the oven for about 4 hours at 160°C.

2 To make pasta dough: make a well with flour, add eggs to centre, mix well until smooth paste, wrap in cling film and place in fridge for 30 minutes.

3 Skin and deseed tomatoes for chutney, finely chop shallot.

4 Sweat shallots, add tomatoes, tomato paste, sugar, mushrooms and red wine vinegar for 2 minutes.

5 Cut leeks into approx. 4-cm pieces.

6 Cook the leeks in the stock (5 minutes), strain and finish with butter and cream.

7 Reduce stock by half, add foie gras, cream and blitz.

8 When the oxtail is ready, wrap it in the pasta for the tortellini.

TO SERVE:

Spoon buttered leeks in a round mould in the bowl. Place tortellini on top of leeks. Quenelle (*see glossary*) the tomato chutney and place beside tortellini. Pour foie gras sauce around leeks and drizzle with truffle oil and add some black olives for colour.

Drinks

Chianti Classico, Barolo wine or a white wheat beer, such as Erdinger Weissbier or O'Hara's Curim (Gold) Celtic Wheat Beer.

FISH

NEVEN MAGUIRE

A Study of Shellfish

'This dish has the perfect balance of texture and flavour from the selection of shellfish. It's a wonderful showcase for the fantastic produce that is harvested from the Irish ocean.' *Neven Maguire*

Serves 6

For the Crispy Prawns in Kataifi Pastry:

150g frozen kataifi pastry

25g plain flour

Sea salt and freshly ground black pepper

1 egg

50ml milk

12 fresh Dublin Bay prawns, peeled and veins removed

Groundnut oil, for deep-frying

Chilli jam, to serve

Curried mayonnaise, to serve

TO PREPARE THE PRAWNS:

1   Thaw the pastry while still in its plastic for a minimum of 2 hours before using. Once thawed it will be soft and pliable and ready to use, but remember when using it that you must always keep it well covered.

2   Place the flour in a shallow dish and season generously. Beat the egg with the milk and a pinch of salt in a separate shallow dish.

3   Toss the prawns in the seasoned flour until lightly coated, then dip briefly in the egg wash, then wrap well in kataifi pastry. To wrap the prawns, lay about 10g of the kataifi pastry in a rectangle on a board. Sit a prawn across the width at the end closest to you and then roll it up away from you to completely enclose it. Place on non-stick parchment paper, spaced well apart so that they don't get tangled up and cover with cling film. Chill until ready to use (these will sit happily for up to 4 hours in the fridge).

For the Crab Ravioli:

100g organic salmon fillet, skinned,
  boned and cubed

1 egg yolk

1 tbsp cold cream

Sea salt and freshly ground black
  pepper

1 tsp snipped fresh chives

1 tsp chopped fresh basil

100g white crab meat

12 wonton wrappers

Egg wash (made with 1 egg and
  1 tbsp milk), to glaze

Creamed leeks, to serve

For the Oysters:

6 Pacific oysters

1 rindless smoked streaky bacon
  rasher

Knob of butter

50g spinach leaves, washed and
  tough stalks removed

3 tbsp flaked sea salt

Lemongrass foam, to serve

For the Scallops:

6 king scallops, roes removed (these
  can be saved for another dish) and
  patted dry with kitchen paper

1 tbsp rapeseed oil

Juice of ½ lemon

Sea salt and freshly ground black
  pepper

Sauce vierge (see page 35), to serve

TO MAKE THE RAVIOLI:

1 Blend the salmon in a food processor. Add the egg yolk. Next add the cream, season to taste and blend to a smooth consistency. Place in a bowl, stir in chives and basil, then fold in the crab.

2 Lay out the wonton wrappers on a work surface. Brush one wrapper with a little of the egg wash. Place a spoonful of the crab mixture in the centre and place another wonton wrapper on top. Shape and seal well. Using a 6-cm scone cutter, cut to give a neat finish. Blanch in a pan of boiling salted water for 2 minutes, remove with a slotted spoon and refresh in a bowl of iced water. Arrange on a tray and chill until needed.

TO PREPARE THE OYSTERS:

Scrub the oyster shells. Place one, wrapped in a clean tea towel, on a firm surface with the flattest shell uppermost and the hinge pointing towards you. Grip firmly, insert an oyster knife into the gap in the hinge and twist to snap the shells apart. Slide the blade along the inside of the upper shell to sever the muscle that keeps the shells together. Lift the lid off the top shell and run the knife under the oyster to remove it from the shell. Repeat until all the oysters are taken out of their shells. Reserve the bottom half of the shells for presentation.

TO PREPARE THE SCALLOPS:

Sear the scallops in rapeseed oil over a high heat for 1 minute on each side, until golden and crispy. Transfer to a plate, add a squeeze of lemon juice, then season to taste.

TO FINISH THE PRAWNS:

Heat the oil in a deep-fat fryer or a deep-sided pan to 160°C. Cook in batches of three for about 3 minutes, turning halfway through, until crisp and golden brown and the prawns are cooked through. Drain on kitchen paper.

For the Lemongrass Foam:
(makes about 300ml)

1 tsp butter, softened

1 shallot, finely chopped

1 lemongrass stalk, outer leaves
  removed and the core halved

1 lemon, finely grated rind and juice

50ml dry white wine

200ml coconut milk

100ml vegetable stock

Sea salt and freshly ground white
  pepper

1 tsp soya lecithin

Chef's Tip

Cook ahead. The scallops can be
opened and placed on damp kitchen
roll in the fridge for up to 3–4 days.
The prawns can be wrapped in the
pastry and chilled for up to 3–4 days.
The crab ravioli can be made 2–3
days in advance and covered with
cling film in the fridge. All these
elements can be frozen.

Drinks

Sancerre, Muscadet, Champagne,
Albariño wines or a Pilsner lager, such
as Czech Pilsner Urquell, Belgian
Estaminet, Indian Kingfisher or
CloughMore Granite Lager.

TO MAKE THE LEMONGRASS FOAM:

Melt butter in pan, add shallot, lemongrass, lemon rind
and cook for 2-3 minutes, until softened. Add wine and
reduce by half. Stir in coconut milk and stock and bring to
boil, simmer until thickened. Discard lemongrass, season
to taste and blend. Sieve into a pan, keep warm, add soya.
Before serving use a hand blender to create a foam.

TO FINISH THE CRAB RAVIOLI:

Place in a pan of boiling salted water for 2 minutes to just
warm through, then drain briefly on kitchen paper.

TO FINISH THE OYSTERS:

Grill the bacon until crisp. Drain on kitchen paper. Melt the
butter in a pan over a medium heat, add the spinach and a
pinch of salt. Cook for a minute or so, stirring occasionally,
until just wilted. Drain off any excess liquid and then
spoon a small mound into each reserved oyster shell.
Arrange on a warmed plate and keep warm. Add the raw
oysters to the warm lemongrass foam and gently poach
for 30 seconds. Carefully remove the oysters with a slotted
spoon and place on top of the spinach in the oyster shells.

TO SERVE:

Add the chilli jam and mayonnaise onto warmed plates
and arrange the prawns in Kataifi pastry on top. Spoon
the creamed leeks onto the plates and place the ravioli
on top. Place each oyster shell on flaked sea salt, crumble
over the smoked streaky bacon, then spoon over the
lemongrass foam. Add the sauce vierge and place a
seared scallop on top.

MICHAEL O'MEARA

Red Mullet & Fried Prawns with Salt & Vinegar Squid Ink Sauce

'This dish showcases the delicate, yet deep-flavoured and vibrant red mullet, with the black squid ink sauce providing the perfect contrast. Texture comes from the crisp fried common prawns – among the best-flavoured foods from Irish waters.' *Michael O'Meara*

Serves 2

2 one-portion-sized red mullets, (each 300-350g weight), gutted, de-scaled with pin bones and heads removed. The fish should be filleted in such a way that the tail is left intact.

10 live common prawns

1 large Maris Piper potato, peeled

60g sea beet leaves

5g squid ink

25ml good quality balsamic vinegar

10g Japanese mirin sweet sake

½ tsp thick and easy smart starch (available in chemists)

10ml extra virgin olive

25g flour

Salt and freshly milled black pepper, to season

1 Place the balsamic vinegar into a stainless steel saucepan and reduce by a third. Remove from the heat, add the squid ink, mirin and a very small pinch of salt. Thicken the sauce by sprinkling and whisking in a small amount of the thick and easy starch and set aside.

2 Prepare the potatoes with a spiralator tool and deep fry until crisp, place aside.

3 Season the red mullet with a little salt and black pepper and rub with olive oil. Place onto a non-stick oven tray and bake in a moderate oven at 160°C for about 10 minutes or until the fish just begins to flake apart.

4 Dredge the prawns in flour and deep fry until crispy.

5 Toss the sea beet in a hot pan with a little olive oil until it begins to wilt. No need to season as it is naturally salty.

TO SERVE:
Place the red mullet onto a pre-warmed plate. Place the crisp potatoes onto the fish and garnish with the crisp prawns. Place the sea beet into the centre of the fish and drizzle the squid ink sauce around the plate. A few drops of good olive oil can also be lightly drizzled around the plate.

Drinks
Riesling and Gewürztraminer wines or Pilsner lager.

STEPHEN MCALLISTER

Earl Grey Tea-Cured Salmon with Apple, Cucumber, Yogurt & Dill

'This salmon recipe has always been a big hit with the customers of The Pig's Ear. It is also a great dinner party starter as all the work is done ahead of time leaving you free to mingle with your guests.' *Stephen McAllister*

Serves 4

500g organic Irish salmon, skin off
  & pin-boned
Zest of 1 orange & 1 lemon
70g sea salt
90g sugar
30g dill or fennel
Tea from 2 Earl Grey tea bags
100g yogurt, strained in a muslin
  cloth overnight
1 Granny Smith apple, sliced into
  crescent shapes
1 cucumber, one half sliced thinly
  length ways, seasoned with salt to
  soften; the other peeled and cut
  into 4 disks, with the remainder
  scooped out into little balls using
  a small melon baller
Fennel herb, for garnish

1 Add the orange, lemon, salt, sugar, dill and tea to a bowl.
2 Cover the fish completely with the salt and sugar mixture and place onto a dish.
3 Cover the dish with clingfilm and refrigerate for up to 24 hrs, turning halfway through.
4 When the curing time is up, wash under running cold water. Pat dry using a cloth.
5 Place on a chopping board and slice into even pieces.
6 Take the yogurt from the cloth and season with salt and white pepper to taste.
7 Lay the cucumber slices on a board overlapping slightly. Spoon some yogurt in the centre and roll up into a cigar shape. Repeat until you have four cucumber rolls.
8 Place a slice of salmon on each plate with the different cucumbers beside it. Top with some apple slices and a little fennel herb. Finish with olive oil and a squeeze of lemon.

Drinks

German Riesling (Kabinett) wine or a Pilsner lager such as Czech Budjovicky Budvar; O'Hara's Irish Lager, Helles Style.

SEAN HOGAN

Dublin Bay Prawns with Pernod

'When the infamous absinthe was banned in France by government decree in 1915, one of its chief manufacturers, Henri Pernod, began making a more acceptable, lower strength alcoholic drink. With its aniseed flavour and without the offending wormwood of its predecessor, Pernod was created. This recipe marries Pernod with delicious fresh Dublin Bay prawns.' *Sean Hogan*

Serves 4

600g Dublin Bay prawns, shelled
  and de-veined
1 tbsp olive oil
25g butter
200ml double cream
70ml Pernod
Salt and cayenne pepper
2 cups of cooked rice

1 Season the Dublin Bay prawns with salt.
2 Heat your pan with 1 tbsp olive oil and the butter.
3 Add the Dublin Bay prawns.
4 Toss the Dublin Bay prawns in the pan for approximately 1 minute.
5 Add Pernod (the alcohol may flame).
6 Drain off any excess oil from the pan.
7 Add the double cream and reduce until the cream thickens to sauce-like texture.

TO SERVE:
Serve on a bed of cooked rice. Dust slightly with cayenne pepper.

Variation
Add mushrooms, shallots, garlic if desired to enhance the flavours and overall taste of the dish.

Drinks
Chablis or New Zealand Sauvignon Blanc wines or a pale lager such as Cloughmore Granite Lager.

Killala Bay Chowder

'Chowders are found all over the world, though the origin of the word may stem from Cornwall. The dish was traditionally thickened with "hardtack" or "ship's biscuit". Today flour is often used, although this recipe uses potato to give the chowder body.' *Diarmuid Cawley*

Serves 4

For the Base Soup:

1.5 litres of fresh fish stock (either bought or made with white fish bones)

3-4 medium-sized peeled potatoes, chopped

2 sticks of celery, de-stringed and finely sliced

2 medium-sized white onions, diced

1 medium-sized leek (use mainly the white), finely sliced

¼ of a turnip (swede), chopped

Half glass of dry white wine or Fino sherry

For the Chowder:

Knob of butter

8-12 mussels

8-12 small clams or cockles

4 crab claws

200g salmon tail (no skin or fat), diced

200g meaty white fish – monkfish/ halibut/cod – diced

Measure of Cognac

Pouring cream

Chopped parsley, to finish

TO MAKE THE BASE SOUP:

1 Soften the onion, leek, celery and turnip in some butter on a low to medium heat but do not brown or darken the colour.

2 Add the potatoes, season with salt and pepper. At this point add the chosen wine and reduce it slightly for a few more minutes then add the stock. Cover and simmer on a low heat until the potato is very tender.

3 Remove from the heat and blend into a fine purée to make a thin soup. Taste and correct the seasoning. It should taste similar to leek and potato soup but with the flavour of fish stock. This base soup can be made in advance and stored in the fridge for two days.

TO MAKE THE CHOWDER:

1 On a medium heat, in a wide, deep pan, melt a knob of butter. Add the diced fish, shellfish and crab. Increase the heat and sauté for about 1 minute. Do not cook fully as the fish will begin to break up.

2 Add the cognac to the hot pan and if possible flambé. Otherwise, allow the alcohol to simmer off. The cognac adds a distinct element to the dish but the alcohol needs to burn off. As soon as the flame dies down, add a large ladle of base soup per person.

3 Allow the chowder to heat up and simmer. As the shellfish open, add the cream (it can be a dash or a lot!) and reduce further to get the right consistency. Be careful not to overcook the fish.

4 Add plenty of chopped parsley and serve immediately.

Variation

Many types of fish are interchangeable in this dish. Add smoked haddock for that distinctive smoked and salty taste or experiment with what is fresh at the market. However, oily fish such as mackerel, herring and sardines are not suitable.

Chef's Tip

The trick to making this chowder taste delicious is to use quality fresh fish stock and add the fish near the finishing stage to prevent overcooking. For the stock, use only fresh, white fish bones. Sole, turbot and brill work best.

Drinks

Samuel Adams light beer or light Chardonnay wine.

DIARMUID MURPHY

Pan-Fried Mackerel in Porridge Oats

'Mackerel is is a cheap, nutritious and sustainable fish. This dish requires few ingredients and is perfect for impromptu lunches or light suppers. All fishmongers and most supermarkets will have mackerel. You can use whole mackerel but you will need to put the whole mackerel in a pre-heated oven, 170ºC, for about three minutes.' *Diarmuid Murphy*

Serves 2

4 mackerel fillets, skin-on, boned
40ml olive or Irish rapeseed oil
50g Irish porridge oats
Salt and pepper

1 Pour the porridge oats into a shallow dish and dip the mackerel fillets into the oats. Make sure you coat both sides of each fillet and gently press the oats on to the fish.
2 Heat a cast-iron frying pan with olive or rapeseed oil.
3 Place the fillets skin side down and cook until crisp and they have a little colour.
4 Turn over the fillets and repeat for about 45 seconds.
5 Remove the fillets from the pan and place on kitchen paper to remove any excess oil. Serve immediately.

Chef's Tip
For added pleasure, you can put 50g of good Irish butter in to the pan at the last minute. Suggestions for serving include: warm potato and dill salad, beetroot and carrot slaw, spinach and wild garlic salad, horseradish mayonnaise, and tomato relish.

Drinks
Muscadet sur Lie wine or a Pilsner lager such as Locavore Blonde, Wicklow Wolf Brewing, Bray.

DIARMUID MURPHY

Tataki of Tuna

'Atlantic bluefin tuna are caught off the west coast of Ireland, and whilst the largest end up in Japanese markets, we often see this fantastic fish landed and it is available at good fish counters and at fishmongers.'
Diarmuid Murphy

Serves 2

200g tuna loin, trimmed
40ml rapeseed oil
Salt and black pepper

1 Slice the tuna into two pieces. Heat a griddle pan until very hot.
2 Brush the tuna with the rapeseed oil and season well with salt and pepper.
3 Sear for 15-20 seconds on all sides, plunge into ice cold water to arrest the cooking process and immediately pat dry.

TO SERVE:
Cut into slices and arrange on a plate. Serve with a good quality soy sauce and Wasabi for dipping, or strong mustard, or pickled ginger, or a small green salad with some bread.

Drinks
Manzanilla Sherry, sake, Lapsang Souchong tea or a Pilsner lager, such as Tiger Beer from Singapore, or Sunbeam Pilsner, from Rising Sons Brewery, Cork.

MAINS

Andalucían Beef Casserole

'This simple beef stew is an ideal dish for those cold winter days, keep things simple to ensure a satisfying result.'
James Carberry

Serves 4

500g shin beef, cut in 50g pieces
20g smoked paprika
25g flour
20g butter
20ml olive oil
10g garlic
100g shallot
5g red chilli
30g tomato purée
200ml white wine
300ml brown stock
Sprig of thyme

1 Mix together the flour and smoked paprika and season with salt and freshly ground black pepper. Toss the cubes of beef in the dry mix so all surfaces are covered.

2 Colour the beef gently in a frying pan in the olive oil and butter. You may need to do this in batches. Do not overcrowd the pan with beef. Remove the beef from the pan and set aside.

3 Sauté the shallot, garlic and chilli in the leftover fat. Do not colour. Add the tomato purée.

4 Put the beef back in the pan. Add the white wine and stock to just barely cover the meat and bring to the boil.

5 Cover with a parchment paper and metal lid and place into a preheated oven.

6 Cook in the oven at 165°C until tender, 2 to 3 hours. When tender correct the sauce if necessary and season if required.

TO SERVE:
Serve with rice or a rice pilaff and a tossed salad.

Drinks
Oloroso Sherry, Côtes du Rhône or Rioja wines, or a stout, such as Porterhouse Wrasslers XXXX Stout, Murphy's or Guinness Irish Stout.

Bellingham Blue, Chestnut, Spinach & Wild Mushroom Tart

'Perfect for lunch or dinner, this vegetarian dish blends a wonderful mix of rich Irish ingredients. It makes either four individual tartlets or one larger one, using a 20cm fluted or plain pan.'

Diarmaid Murphy

Serves 4-6

For the Pastry:

300g plain flour, plus a little extra for dusting

150g butter

Salt and white pepper for seasoning

2-3 tbsp cold water

2 eggs

150ml single cream

150ml milk

Salt and white pepper for seasoning

For the Filling:

50g butter

30g shallots, diced

200g wild mixed mushrooms, quartered

100g tinned chestnuts, chopped

150g Bellingham Blue cheese

A handful of spinach leaves, torn

For the Salad:

100g rocket

100g raw organic beetroot, cut into thin strips

A squeeze of lemon juice

2 tbsp of olive oil

Salt and white pepper for seasoning

100g cherry tomatoes, halved

Preheat the oven to 190°C.

TO MAKE THE PASTRY:

1 Tip the flour into a food processor with the butter and pulse until the mixture resembles breadcrumbs. Add the cold water and blend again until the dough comes together. Turn out onto a lightly floured surface and briefly knead.

2 Roll out the pastry and line pan, leaving excess pastry to allow for shrinkage. Line the pastry with greaseproof paper and fill with uncooked rice. Bake for 15 minutes, then remove the paper and rice and continue cooking until crisp and light golden. Using a knife, carefully trim off excess pastry and discard.

Chef's Tip

If you cannot source Bellingham Blue cheese, Cashel Blue or Stilton cheese would also be highly recommended.

Drinks

A light to medium-bodied dry wine such as a Sauvignon Blanc or a pale ale or Pilsner beer.

TO MAKE THE FILLING:

1 Add the butter to a hot pan over a medium heat, add the shallots and mushrooms and cook until soft. Add the spinach and chestnuts and cook for a further minute. Allow mixture to cool.

2 Lightly whisk the eggs, then whisk in the cream and milk. Season with salt and pepper, then stir in the cooked vegetable mixture.

3 Pour into the pastry case and bake for 25-30 minutes until puffed and golden.

FOR THE SALAD:

Lightly toss all ingredients together and serve as a small cluster mounded on top of the tart.

Celtic Steak

'What makes this Celtic recipe special is the flavour of the Jameson Irish whiskey. To make it even more special, try it flambé style – it's not as difficult as you might think.' *Sean Hogan*

Serves 4

4 x 225g Irish sirloin steaks

100g onion, diced

100g mushrooms, sliced

50g butter

200ml double cream

70 ml Irish whiskey (Jameson)

Salt and black pepper

Olive oil

Irish mustard

Worcestershire sauce (Lea and Perrins)

1 Place the steak between sheets of clingfilm and beat gently until thin as this will reduce the cooking time.

2 Coat the steak with the mustard, salt and black pepper.

3 Heat your pan with 1 tbsp olive oil and butter.

4 Add the diced onion, sliced mushrooms and sweat, without colouring, until cooked.

5 Remove the mushrooms and onion from the pan.

6 Add the steak to the same hot pan, cook on both sides to liking.

7 Add the cooked onions and mushrooms to the pan.

8 Add the Irish whiskey and flambé if you wish, but be careful. Add Worcestershire sauce to taste.

9 Add the double cream, reduce and serve.

Variation

Substitute fillet of beef, pork or chicken if you prefer or why not add garlic and sliced red peppers and serve with delicious creamed potatoes.

Drinks

Californian Cabernet Sauvignon wine, or an Irish Stout such as Guinness, or an Irish Red Ale such as O'Hara's Leann Folláin.

Celeriac Baked in Barley & Fermented Hay with Hazelnuts & Smoked Celeriac Tea

Included here to show the skills and inventiveness of Mark Moriarty, a DIT graduate and S. Pellegrino 2015 World's Best Young Chef, this exciting and challenging dish is not one to be attempted easily at home.

Serves 10

For the Barley Crust:

350g rye flour

130g salt

80g T45 French flour

150g egg white, may need more – judge by eye, dough needs to be pliable

For the Barley Miso (quick version):

100g barley, toasted

20g Japanese miso

Large handful hay, dried & thermomixed into powder

For the Baked Celeriac:

2 celeriacs, peeled, halved & trimmed to natural shape

100g barley crust

20g barley miso

TO MAKE THE BARLEY CRUST:

Place all the dry ingredients in a Kenwood mixer and mix to a dry but pliable consistency, roll out approx. 3mm thick.

TO MAKE THE BARLEY MISO:

1 Place the barley in a preheated oven at 200°C for 20 minutes, until toasted.

2 Cook in salted water until soft.

3 Drain and add to blender along with the hay and blitz to a pulp.

4 Once cooled to a lukewarm temperature, add the miso and mix thoroughly.

TO MAKE THE BAKED CELERIAC:

1 Blowtorch the trimmed celeriac until blackened, marinate in the barley miso and leave overnight.

2 Roll out the barley crust and cover it with the barley miso.

3 Place the baked celeriac on top of the hay and begin to wrap the crust around it until perfectly smooth parcels are achieved.

4 Bake the parcels at 200°C for 40 minutes. Remove and open tableside.

For the Pickled Celeriac Sheet:

1 whole celeriac, peeled

50g water

50g white wine vinegar

20g chopped celeriac

50g sugar

For the Hazelnut Emulsion:

10g Dijon mustard

10g white wine vinegar

30g pasteurised egg yolk

500ml hazelnut oil

For the Toasted Hazelnuts:

10g peeled hazelnuts

For the Crispy Celeriac:

½ celeriac, blitzed to a fine crumb in thermomix

300ml vegetable oil

TO MAKE THE PICKLED CELERIAC SHEET:

1 Using a Japanese mandolin, turn the celeriac into sheets, trim the edges and place in a vacuum bag.

2 Heat the water, vinegar, chopped celeriac and sugar until dissolved and place a small amount in the vacuum bags. Compress the sheets and set aside for service.

TO MAKE THE HAZELNUT EMULSION:

Place the mustard, vinegar and egg yolk in a thermomix and blitz at speed 4. Emulsify with the hazelnut oil and place in a squeezie bottle.

TO PREPARE THE TOASTED HAZELNUTS:

Place the hazelnuts on a tray in an oven at 200°C for 10 minutes, until golden brown.

TO MAKE THE CRISPY CELERIAC:

1 Add the oil and celeriac to a pot and place on an induction hob.

2 Bring to the boil before reducing heat to a simmer.

3 Stir constantly until celeriac turns golden brown, remove and dry on paper.

For the Celeriac Tea:

400ml raw celeriac juice

30g toasted hay

To Garnish:

Celery leaves

TO MAKE THE CELERIAC TEA:

1 Bring the raw celeriac juice slowly to the boil in a pot, skimming regularly. When it reaches the boil, remove from the heat, and pass the liquid through a muslin cloth.

2 Place 20g of the toasted hay into the tea and infuse for 30 seconds before passing through a muslin cloth again. Pour the tea into a cast-iron kettle and stuff the lid with 10g of hay; light this on fire before placing the lid on, in order to lightly smoke the hay, and serve tableside.

TO GARNISH:

Remove the sweet light green/yellow leaves from the celery head to use as garnish.

Drinks

Guinness or Gewürztraminer wine.

MARK FARRELL

Chicken Satay

'This Indonesian dish is a family favourite. The combination of nuts, coconut and chillies hits all the right notes. For an authentic Asian experience, use fresh limes, lemongrass and coriander.' *Mark Farrell*

Serves 4

2-4 Manor Farm chicken breasts, diced

100g pineapple, diced

100g red pepper, diced

8 wooden skewers

Glug peanut oil

1 stick lemongrass, chopped finely

1 small onion, diced

½ tsp cumin seeds

400ml unsweetened coconut milk

150g peanuts, chopped

5ml fish sauce

50g fresh coriander, chopped

25g red chillies, chopped

10g garlic, chopped

10g ginger, chopped

Freshly squeezed lime juice

Honey

1 Arrange chicken, pineapple and peppers on the skewers. Season with salt and pepper just prior to cooking.

2 Add the oil to a hot pan and toss each skewer quickly in the oil to colour.

3 Remove and put in a hot oven (180°C) to cook through for approximately 8 minutes.

4 To the same hot pan add the onion, lemongrass and cumin seeds, cook without colour.

5 Add the coconut milk and bring to a light simmer. Add the peanuts and fish sauce, simmer and remove from heat. Add the chillies, garlic, ginger, coriander. Season to your taste with lime juice and honey.

TO SERVE:
Combine the sauce with the hot, cooked chicken skewers. They can be served as a hors d'oeuvre or combined with noodles or rice as a main dish.

Variation
Peanut butter and chicken stock can be used instead of peanuts and coconut milk. Palm sugar can be used as an alternative to honey for a more authentic dish.

Drinks
German Riesling wine or a brown ale, such as Belgian Steenbrugge Bruin, Irish Coalface Black IPA or Kentucky IPA from Alltech.

Chef's Tip
The chicken can be marinated in some of the coconut milk as an additional flavour enhancer. A few tablespoons of chicken stock will thin the sauce if it thickens too much on holding before serving.

Crispy Pork with Thyme Stuffing

'A dish to remind us of the pleasure, economy and quality which can be devised from simple ingredients. It is so convenient to buy ready-stuffed meat and poultry, but the taste of homemade stuffing with fresh thyme is hard to beat.' *Mark Farrell*

Serves 4

1 small onion, diced

50g butter

1 eating apple, such as a Granny Smith, diced

20 walnuts, shelled

1 bunch of fresh thyme leaves, chopped

400g fresh white breadcrumbs

Freshly chopped parsley

100g streaky bacon

800g pork fillet, trimmed

25g icing sugar

1　Combine the onion and butter in a hot, thick-bottomed pan and cook till transparent, season. Add the apple and 8 diced walnuts to the pan. Mix and remove from heat. Combine with the thyme leaves and allow to cool. Add the breadcrumbs and parsley, mix and set aside.

2　Cut the pork fillet lengthways. Place between two sheets of cling film and beat gently with a rolling pin to flatten into an even wider piece.

3　Lay the bacon pieces lengthways on another sheet of cling film. Overlap the bacon slightly to create a carpet on the film. Remove the pork from the cling film and place on the bacon carpet. Flatten into place, and then put the stuffing mixture on top. Roll the bacon, pork and stuffing together like a Swiss roll. Place on a buttered tray and roast in a moderate oven for approximately 30 minutes or until cooked through. Remove and allow to rest.

4　Dredge the remaining walnuts in icing sugar and warm under a hot grill and place onto warmed plates. Carve the rested pork onto the plate and served with potatoes and vegetables accompanied by gravy.

Drinks

Rioja or Beaujolais Cru wines or a craft cider, such as McIvor's Irish Cider, Traditional Dry, Falling Apple Cider, or Suffolk Cyder's Aspall Dry Premier Cru.

Variation

You can use pear instead of apple and the walnuts could be replaced by hazelnuts or pistachio. Wholegrain mustard, freshly chopped tarragon and honey combined in the gravy would also help to deliver a real opulent feast.

DERRY CLARKE

Crispy Duck Breast & Butternut Squash

'This duck recipe is simple and tasty. The dish can be adapted for a chicken breast, but the chicken needs to be cooked through.' *Derry Clarke*

Serves 4

For the Butternut Squash & Duck Breast:

4 duck breast

1 butternut squash, peeled and cubed

200g cured bacon, cut, blanched and cubed

4 large shallots, peeled and halved

1 tbsp honey

Juice 1 orange

Juice 1 lime

1 tbsp olive oil

50g butter

50g fresh sage, chopped

50g fresh thyme, chopped

Sea salt and cracked black pepper

For the Star Anise Jus:

250ml demi glaze or beef stock

4 star anise, lightly crushed

2 oranges, juice and zest

100g brown sugar

100ml red wine vinegar

TO PREPARE THE BUTTERNUT SQUASH & DUCK BREAST:

1 Put butternut squash, shallots and bacon in a bowl. Add orange, lime, olive oil, butter, sage and thyme, season with sea salt and cracked black pepper.

2 Toss all the ingredients together, spread onto a roasting tray and bake at 180°C until tender, about 15-20 minutes.

3 Put duck breast, skin side down, on a cold heavy frying pan.

4 Place on high heat until crisp, 5 minutes. Turn duck breast over, reduce heat, and cook for a further 3-5 minutes, to allow the duck to cook pink.Cook longer for medium and well done. Allow the duck breast to rest.

TO MAKE THE STAR ANISE JUS:

1 Heat sugar and vinegar over a medium heat to form a brown caramel. Do not overcook as your sauce will be bitter.

2 Add the orange juice, star anise and demi glaze or beef stock. Simmer for 5 minutes. Strain, season and add zest.

TO SERVE:

Carve the duck breast lengthways. Spoon the vegetables onto serving plates x 4. Place duck on top and serve star anise jus on the side.

Drinks

Pinot Noir wine or an amber ale, such as Donegal's Devil's Backbone Amber Ale, or Thwaites Black Sheep Ale or Double Century, from Lancashire.

MÁIRTÍN MAC CON IOMAIRE

Dublin Coddle

'A quintessential Dublin dish which is similar to Irish Stew but uses rashers and sausages in place of lamb or mutton. This version is slightly upmarket as it includes leek and cream to enrich the dish.'

Máirtín Mac Con Iomaire

Serves 4

500g sausages, cocktail sausages
  work well

500g rashers, cut in chunks

500g onion, cut in chunks

1kg potatoes, cut in chunks

1kg carrot, peeled and cut in chunks

½ leek, finely sliced, using green and
  white of leek

1 litre chicken stock or water

100ml cream

Seasoning, mostly ground pepper as
  little salt is required due to salt in
  meat and stock

1 Add all ingredients, except leeks, seasoning and cream, into a pot and bring to the boil.

2 Reduce heat and simmer for 25 minutes.

3 Skim any impurities that rise to the top.

4 Add the cream and the chopped leeks and cook for a further 3 minutes, season and serve.

Drinks

O'Hara's Irish Red Ale, Irish Stout, Porter or Kentucky Barrel Stout from Alltech.

DERMOT SEBERRY

Flavours of Lamb

'This lamb dish of slow-braised shoulder and marinated rump with smoked potato, crunchy breaded cheese fritter and spinach purée is aimed at the skilled cook.' *Dermot Seberry*

Serves 4

For the Lamb Shoulder Sausage:

1kg lamb shoulder

100g sliced pancetta or Parma ham

100g each of onion, leek, carrot & celeriac, diced

2 garlic cloves

1 branch of rosemary

100ml white wine

500ml chicken stock

TO MAKE THE LAMB SHOULDER SAUSAGE:

1 On a wide-based pan, sear the shoulder till brown all over and place it in a deep roasting tray or casserole dish with the roughly chopped vegetables.

2 Add the white wine with enough boiling chicken stock to a depth of 4 cm.

3 Cover the roasting tray or dish tightly with foil/lid and roast at 150°C for 3 hours, checking every 30 minutes that the liquid does not evaporate. Top up if needed. When cooked, it should be 'falling apart' tender. Reserve the pan juices for the gravy.

4 Using 2 forks, rake the meat into a bowl.

5 Lay down a double layer of cling wrap, 120cm x 120cm.

6 Layer strips of overlapping pancetta or Parma ham on the cling wrap. Spoon the flaked lamb, 4-cm thick, across the ham. Lift the cling wrap and roll one end of the ham all the way forward over the flaked lamb, packing it tightly, to form a long sausage shape, always keeping the cling wrap on the outside. Complete the sausage shape by twisting both ends of the cling wrap tightly. Tie the ends and leave this in the fridge for 1 hour to set.

7 To portion this roll, simply cut through the cling wrap at 4-6 cm intervals. Remove the cling wrap and panfry the outer layer of ham till brown. Then place into the oven at 140°C for 10 minutes to reheat the inside.

For the Lamb Rump & Marinade:

1 lamb rump steak (400g), fat trimmed

100ml port

100ml balsamic vinegar

2 tbsp soy sauce

1 tbsp honey

5 garlic cloves, crushed

A sprig of fresh thyme

For the Spinach Purée:

1 large handful of spinach

1 knob of butter

1 tsp blue cheese, grated

100ml chicken or vegetable stock

1 tbsp mashed potato

For the Rosemary Gravy:

500ml boiling water,

1 tbsp rosemary spines,

1 tbsp ketchup,

1 jellied chicken stock cube

10g gravy granules

Drinks

Rioja or St Emilion Bordeaux wines, Guinness Black Lager, or a pale ale such as Howling Gale Irish Pale Ale, from Cork.

TO COOK THE LAMB RUMP:

1 Mix together all the marinade ingredients. Marinate the rump steak for 2 hours.

2 20 minutes before serving, sear the rumps on a pan, fat side down, to render/melt off any excess fat. Then season the meat, seal on a pan and cook at 180°C for 15 minutes.

3 Remove from the oven and rest the meat in foil for 10 minutes while you reheat the other components.

4 For lamb rump, 'medium' is a nicer texture to eat as the natural fibres are chewier if any way rare.

TO MAKE THE SPINACH PURÉE:

1 In a small pan, sweat the spinach in the butter till wilted. Reserve a spoonful of this for the smoked mash potato later.

2 Add 100ml of chicken stock, 1 tbsp of mash potato and 1 tsp blue cheese.

3 Simmer for 2 minutes. Using a blender, purée all the ingredients to form a smooth, soft green purée.

TO MAKE THE ROSEMARY GRAVY:

1 With the exception of the gravy granules, boil together all the ingredients listed with the reserved roasted juices from the shoulder and 50ml of the rump marinade. Reduce this by half.

2 Finish the sauce by whisking in enough gravy granules to thicken the sauce. Strain and reheat when ready to serve.

Chef's Tip

With the exception of the rump, all components can be cooked a couple of hours in advance and reheated just before serving.

For the Smoked Potato:

4-6 peeled rooster potatoes

2 tbsp green tea

200g raw rice

2 tbsp demerara sugar

2 tbsp of fresh rosemary spines

1 bunch fresh thyme, roughly chopped

Salt and white pepper

For the Cheese Fritters:

200g blue goat's cheese

200g flour

2 beaten eggs

200g dried breadcrumbs

Optional Garnish:

Serve with a sprig of rosemary, some redcurrants, micro herbs and a band of pancetta. (Pancetta band: wrap a slice of pancetta around a well-oiled metal cutter and place in the oven at 130°C for 15 minutes till set and crispy. Slide the ring off the cutter.) Secure the pancetta band on top of the tube using a spot of mash or reduced sticky jus.

TO MAKE THE SMOKED POTATO:

1 Roughly chop the potatoes into 2cm dice, and boil or steam till soft.

2 Mix together the smoke ingredients. Place them in a wok lined with foil. Cover with a lid, and then heat until heavy smoke builds up inside. Turn the heat off.

3 Place the cooked chunks of potato on a trivet/wire rack suitable to fit under the lid. Lift the lid swiftly and place the potatoes into the wok, covering tightly again to retain as much smoke as possible. Keep covered, off the heat, for 15 minutes.

4 When the fuming is complete, remove the potatoes to a small pot, season with salt, white pepper and add a knob of butter.

5 Mash the potatoes while hot and add the reserved wilted spinach.

6 To serve: spoon the mash 2cm high into a shaping ring or scone cutter.

FOR THE CHEESE FRITTERS:

1 Cut the blue goat's cheese into 2cm dice and roll into balls, allowing 3 per portion.

2 Coat each one in flour, followed by beaten egg and then breadcrumbs.

3 Leave to set in the fridge.

4 Just before serving, deep-fry in vegetable oil till crunchy (1 minute).

PLATING THE DISH:

Heat all the components, including your plates. Begin by forming a circle of mash on the plate, followed by a strike of spinach purée across the plate. Place the tube of braised lamb on the plate. Place 3 tiny dots of mash around the plate and place each fritter on top. Slice the rump and layer it across the potato circle. Spoon on enough gravy to complement the meat.

Spicy Creamy Chicken

'This recipe is my favourite chicken dish, which I have prepared throughout my career working in numerous national and international hotels. The dish has always been a best-seller, with customers always requesting the recipe. I hope you enjoy it too.' *George Smith*

Serves 4

800g raw, boned Manor Farm
  chicken, cut into large chunks
75g unsalted butter
2 medium onions, thinly sliced
10g garlic, chopped
2 bay leaves
1 tsp salt
¼ tsp ground black pepper
½ tsp garam masala
½ tsp ground coriander
A pinch of ground turmeric
1 tbsp Worcestershire sauce
75g small mushrooms
175ml double cream

1 In a saucepan melt the butter over a medium heat and add the sliced onion and garlic.
2 Fry until soft and golden brown for approximately 10 minutes.
3 Add the bay leaves and stir fry for about 1 minute.
4 Add the chicken pieces to the onions and lower the heat and continue to fry for another 5 minutes. Add all the spices, seasoning and Worcestershire sauce and continue to stir fry for a further 7-10 minutes, making sure all the chicken pieces are well coated.
5 Add the mushrooms and stir these in, gradually add the cream, mixing all the ingredients well together.
6 Finally, put a lid on and simmer gently over a low heat for about 7-10 minutes, or until the chicken is cooked.

TO SERVE:
Serve with spiced rice and homemade chutney.

Drinks
Riesling, Gewürztraminer or Viognier wines, or an Indian pale ale such as Boundary IPA from Belfast, or Donegal's Scraggy Bar IPA.

Scan the QR code to see George Smith and Frank Cullen in action carving a roast chicken, making a smokey bacon white sauce and plating up for service.

Drinks

Beaujolais Cru or Burgundy Red wines, or an amber
ale, such as Carrig Brazen Amber Ale, from Leitrim, or
Donegal's Devil's Backbone Amber Ale.

GEORGE SMITH

Melody of Guinea Fowl

'This gold-medal winning recipe consists of a smoked breast, stuffed and braised thigh, and roast leg of guinea fowl, all served with thyme and garlic roast potato, celeriac and basil purée, sweet shredded cabbage with bacon and shallots, roast root vegetables and port and truffle jus.' *George Smith*

Serves 4

For the Sauce:

50ml olive oil

100g wild mushrooms, mixed, chopped

100ml apple juice

5g truffles, chopped

20g tarragon, 10g honey

500ml cream, 10g nutmeg

5g salt, 5g pepper, 10g basil

For the Guinea Fowl & Vegetables:

100g apple wood chippings for
  smoking

1 guinea fowl (whole)

200g potatoes, peeled and cut into
  8-cm squares

25g butter

15g sugar

10g thyme, chopped

10g garlic, chopped

200g carrots, parsnip, turnip,
  chopped and blanched

50g shallots, chopped

100g cabbage, chopped

100g celeriac, chopped

50g streaky bacon, diced

½ litre brown stock

50ml port

1 For the sauce: Heat olive oil, sauté the mushrooms, then add apple juice, truffles, tarragon, and honey. Season with salt, pepper and the nutmeg. Finish with cream, reduce for 3 minutes.

2 Portion the guinea fowl into 2 breasts, 2 thighs and 2 legs.

3 Roast bones, cover with stock, bring to the boil, turn down, simmer for 1 hour and strain.

4 Put potatoes in oven with stock for 15 minutes. Drain and salt.

5 Roast legs in oven with potatoes.

6 Braise the thighs in some of the sauce in oven for 15 minutes.

7 Place frying pan on a hot stove, cover with tin foil, place wood chippings on top of tin foil, cover with greaseproof paper and place guinea fowl breasts on top and cook for 6 minutes slowly.

8 Pass stock through a sieve, add port and reduce for 10 minutes, unti jus is ready to serve.

9 Place mushroom and truffle sauce back on heat, add some of the basil, ready to serve.

10 Boil celeriac for 20 minutes and purée with rest of the basil.

11 Roast drained potatoes, blanched vegetables, garlic and thyme in butter and sugar until sticky.

12 Cook and refresh cabbage and add to a hot pan with the bacon and shallots, and cook in butter for 1 minute.

13 Cover with sauce and serve.

Pork Tenderloin with Apricot & Grapefruit Sauce

'This fruity pork dish is packed with vitamins and minerals. Grapefruit and apricots also help lower cholesterol and blood pressure.' *Brona Raftery*

Serves 2

For the Pork:
6 medallions of pork fillet (0.6cm thick)
2 tbsp olive oil

For the Marinade:
Juice and rind of half grapefruit, finely grated
1 heaped tsp brown sugar
1 tbsp olive oil
Salt and black pepper

For the Sauce:
150ml unsweetened apricot purée
300ml chicken stock
8 dried apricots, chopped
Salt and freshly ground black pepper

To Finish:
3 spring onions, finely chopped

1 For the marinade, mix together the juice and rind of the grapefruit, brown sugar, olive oil and seasoning.
2 Marinade the pork in a bowl for 1-2 hours.
3 Remove the pork and drain, reserving the marinade.
4 Heat the olive oil in a pan.
5 Brown the medallions of pork quickly for 2-3 minutes, depending on thickness; turn frequently so they don't burn.
6 Meanwhile, mix the apricot purée with the chicken stock and the reserved marinade.
7 Pour this mixture over the pork, add the chopped apricots, cover the pan and cook till tender, 10-15 minutes on a gentle heat.
8 Chopped spring onion can be added at the end for colour and texture.
9 Taste, correct the seasoning and serve with wholemeal noodles or rice, and a vegetable of your choice.

Drinks
Zinfandel, Grenache wines or Donegal's Devil's Backbone Amber Ale.

Drinks
White Burgundy or a pale ale, such as Waterford's
Metalman Pale Ale, or Graffiti Unfiltered Pale Ale,
Trouble Brewing Company.

BRONA RAFTERY

Roasted Chicken with Orange & Fennel

'This delicious and richly flavoured chicken dish cooks in less than an hour and is perfect comfort food. Removing the skin from the chicken reduces the fat and calorie content.' *Brona Raftery*

Serves 4-6

6 tbsp olive oil

5 tbsp freshly squeezed orange juice

5 tbsp freshly squeezed lemon juice

150ml pernod, sambuca or ouzo (optional)

3 tbsp grain mustard

5 tbsp light brown sugar

2 medium fennel bulbs (500g in total) cut into thin wedges, core removed

1 large Manor Farm or organic chicken, about 1.3kg, divided into 8 pieces, or the same weight in chicken thighs/legs/breasts, on the bone, with the skin removed

6 clementines or 3 small oranges, unpeeled, sliced horizontally into 0.5cm slices

2 tbsp fresh thyme leaves

1 tsp dried fennel seeds, lightly crushed

2 carrots, 2 sticks of celery, cut into small dice

2 red onions, cut into thin wedges

500ml of chicken stock

Salt and black pepper

Cornflour

Chopped flat-leaf parsley, to garnish

1 In a large mixing bowl, whisk together alcohol liqueur (if using), oil, orange and lemon juices, mustard, brown sugar and salt. Season with pepper, to taste. Add fennel, orange slices, carrots, celery, red onions, thyme and crushed fennel seeds. Mix well.

2 If time allows, marinate chicken for several hours or preferably overnight in the fridge.

3 Preheat oven to 220°C. Transfer all ingredients to a large, deep roasting pan. Add the chicken stock to half cover the chicken and vegetables.

4 Roast at a high temperature, until the chicken is browned and cooked through, 35-40 minutes. Remove from the oven.

5 Lift chicken, fennel, vegetables and orange slices onto a large serving plate/dish. Cover and keep warm.

6 Pour the cooking liquid into a saucepan or put the roasting tray back on the hob. Place over a medium heat and bring to a boil.

7 Add two teaspoons of cornflour mixed with four teaspoons of water to thicken the sauce. Bring back to the boil and pour the heated sauce over the chicken. Garnish with parsley and serve with brown rice, bulgar wheat or potatoes.

Chef's Tip

If you are not using the alcohol liqueur, increase the fennel seeds to two teaspoons to intensify the flavour.

Slimmer's Chicken & Vegetable Frittata

'A simple, low carb meal that is a good way to use up leftover picking strips of roast chicken. Consider using locally produced camelina oil, which is extremely high in vitamin E, containing ten times more Omega 3 than olive oil and holds wonderful anti-inflammatory properties.' *Dermot Seberry*

Serves 6

4 large potatoes, sliced

Leftover roast chicken or 2 large
  Manor Farm chicken breasts

8 free-range eggs

Salt, ground white pepper, cayenne
  pepper, to season

1 red onion, 1 white onion, 3 cloves
  of garlic, finely chopped

2 tsp of freshly rubbed thyme

1 red and 1 yellow pepper

Camelina oil (Newgrange Gold)

Drinks

Champagne, Cremant d'Alsace
wine or wheat beer.

1 Place the sliced potatoes on a flat tray with a little water, cover with foil and cook in the oven till semi-soft. 180°C for approximately 25 minutes. Drain and dry in the oven for 5 minutes. A soft, dry texture is ideal.

2 Slice the vegetables and add the cooked chicken. If using raw chicken, slice thinly and toss together with the vegetables in the same bowl. Stir in the thyme and chopped garlic. Reserve some vegetables to use as a top layer for the frittata.

3 Beat the eggs in a jug. Add eggs and potatoes to the main bowl of sliced chicken and vegetables. Season with salt, white pepper and cayenne pepper.

4 Line a 20-cm flan case with parchment paper and brush the base with camelina oil.

5 Cover the base of the flan case with just potato slices, pressing down to release any air pockets and filling gaps with vegetables. Continue by adding the rest of the potato, chicken and vegetable mix, in layers.

6 Top the flan with the reserved vegetables, tossed in a little camelina oil.

7 Bake in an oven for 40 minutes at 110°C. The frittata should be soft but set throughout.

TO SERVE:

Sprinkle liberally with freshly chopped parsley and serve with a dressed beetroot and chickpea salad.

DESSERTS

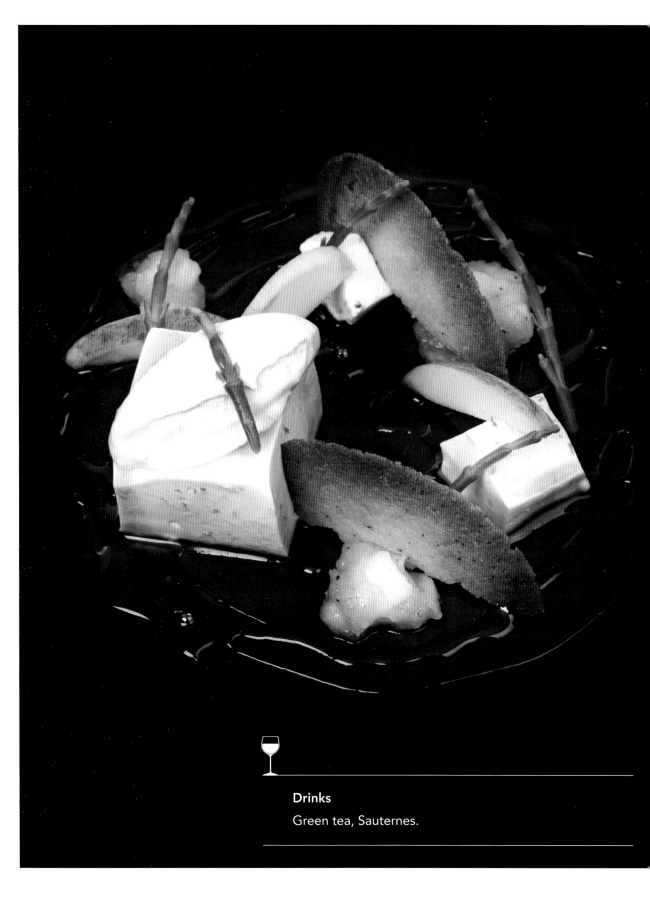

Drinks

Green tea, Sauternes.

MICHAEL O'MEARA

Carrageen Moss Pudding with Apple Ice Cream

'Carrageen moss is a traditional seaweed remedy for respiratory illnesses. The fresh marine undertones of the carrageen pudding are the perfect contrast to a simple apple sauce and apple ice cream. Salty samphire sprigs balance the caramel flavour of the golden syrup.' *Michael O'Meara*

Serves 6

For the Carrageen Pudding:
300ml milk
300ml cream
20g carrageen moss
85ml golden syrup
2 vanilla pods, split and scraped

For the Apple Sauce:
300g apple, peeled and diced small
75g caster sugar

For the Apple Ice Cream:
200g apple sauce (from above batch)
200g crème fraîche
2 tbsp golden syrup

For the Biscuits:
100g caster sugar
220g butter
170g plain white flour

To Finish:
30 sprigs of marsh samphire
18 thin slices of apple
2 tbsp golden syrup

TO MAKE THE CARRAGEEN PUDDING:
In a heavy pot simmer together the cream, milk, golden syrup, carrageen moss and vanilla pod seeds until the liquid begins to thicken, 15-20 minutes. Sieve and pour into non-stick porcelain moulds. Allow to set in the fridge.

TO MAKE THE APPLE SAUCE:
Gently cook the apple and sugar in a heavy pan until the apple begins to break down. Chill in the fridge.

TO MAKE THE APPLE ICE CREAM:
Churn the ice-cream ingredients in an ice-cream machine until smooth and frozen. Set in a deep freeze.

TO MAKE THE BISCUITS:
1 Sieve flour. Mix in sugar. Rub in butter until you have a sand-like texture. Work into a dough and knead lightly. Roll to about 5mm depth and cut into rounds.
2 Place onto a silicone mat-lined baking tray and cook in a pre-heated oven, 180°C, for around 13 minutes, or until the biscuits become a light golden colour.

TO FINISH:
De-mould and place the puddings onto serving plates.
To each dish: add three spoons of apple sauce, the apple slices, biscuits, five sprigs of samphire and drizzle with golden syrup. Finish with a spoon of apple ice cream.

Chocolate & Almond Delights

'These chocolate and almond delights are great as petit fours after a dinner party or as delicious homemade gift-bars wrapped in some cellophane and tied with ribbon.' *John Clancy & Norma Kelly*

Makes 40

150ml double cream

100g butter

½ vanilla pod, split & scraped, to use both pod and seeds

Pinch salt

Pinch bread soda

240g granulated sugar

20g glucose

65ml water

100g 80% dark chocolate

70g whole almonds, roasted & chopped.

1 Bring the cream, butter, vanilla pod and seeds, salt and bread soda to the boil.

2 Chop the dark chocolate into small pieces.

3 Boil the sugar, glucose and water to 145°C.

4 Remove the vanilla pod from the boiled cream. Pour this onto the boiled sugar mix.

5 Mix the chopped chocolate through the caramel and cream mix, heat back up to 118°C.

6 Remove from heat and add the chopped almonds.

7 Pour into moulds or a tray lined with parchment paper and allow to set. The tray can be cut into 2x2cm pieces for petit fours or 3x9cm pieces for bars.

Chef's Tip
To add a marble colour as per the photo, dip the sweets or bars into heated milk, marbled with green-coloured chocolate or green food colouring, allow to set and present in paper cases.

Drinks
Coffee, Imperial Stout, or port.

DARREN HARRIS

Chocolate Beetroot Cake

'The rich, earthy flavour of beetroot adds complexity to dark chocolate which is enhanced by treacly notes from the soft dark brown sugar, all balanced by a little gentle zing from the buttermilk and sour cream. Beetroot is a great antioxidant so you can have your cake and eat it.' *Darren Harris*

Serves 8-10

170g salted butter

150g dark chocolate (90-100 % cocoa)

55g high quality cocoa powder

235g soft flour

4g bread soda

4g baking powder

285g soft dark brown sugar

4 large eggs

230g buttermilk (ideally organic)

245g full fat sour cream

500g fresh raw beetroot, peeled & finely grated (reserve the juice if any)

1 Line a deep, round cake tin with non-stick silicon paper.

2 Melt chocolate and butter in a small pot until it becomes liquid but is still cool to the touch.

3 Combine flour, cocoa powder, bread soda and baking powder. Sieve this mixture 3 times. Add sugar. Finish combining by hand to ensure there are no lumps.

4 Beat eggs vigorously for 2 minutes in a large electrical mixing bowl.

5 Add butter and chocolate mix to sour cream and buttermilk mix. Ensuring this is cool, fold in to the egg mixture.

6 Add all beetroot (and beetroot juice) to this mix and then swirl in 1/3 of the dry ingredients. Once incorporated, add remaining 2/3 of the dry ingredients. Transfer gently to the cake tin and smooth out.

7 Bake at 180°C maximum (fan 165°C) for about 65 minutes. Look for cracks appearing on top of the cake. To see if it is baked, insert a skewer. If it comes out clean, it is ready.

8 Leave to cool in the tin. When almost fully cooled, invert the cake and present smooth side up.

Drinks

Coffee or Black IPA beer.

Chef's Tip

Wear disposable gloves when peeling and preparing the beetroot. Serve finished cake with dark fruits such as blackberries, blueberries and cherries.

MICHEL ROUX SNR

Cherry Clafoutis

'Different fruits can be used in this recipe, according to the season. Plums are always delicious in a clafoutis, particularly greengages.' *Michel Roux Snr*

Serves 6

4 eggs
160g plain flour
160g butter, melted and cooled
300ml milk
120g caster sugar
2 vanilla pods, split lengthways
60g butter
400g ripe cherries, stoned
Granulated sugar, to sprinkle

1 Preheat the oven to 200°C. Lightly beat the eggs in a bowl, with a fork, then lightly beat in the flour. Whisk the cooled melted butter, then gradually whisk in the milk followed by the sugar. Scrape out the seeds from the vanilla pods and add them to the mixture.

2 Cut 20g of the butter into small pieces. Set aside. Use the remaining 40g to generously grease an ovenproof dish, about 22cm in diameter and 3-4cm deep. Spread the cherries evenly over the base of the dish, then pour over the batter mixture.

3 Bake for 10 minutes, and then lower the oven setting to 180°C, and cook for a further 15 minutes or so. Scatter the reserved butter pieces evenly over the top of the clafoutis and bake for another 5 minutes, or until set. To check, carefully insert a knife in the middle; if it comes out clean, the clafoutis is cooked.

4 Sprinkle with granulated sugar and leave to stand for 5 minutes or so. Serve the clafoutis warm, from the baking dish.

Drinks
Monbazillac wine or Kriek beer.

RUTH LAPPIN

Chocolate Tart 'Soufflé' with Black Gypsy Stout Ice Cream

'Although the first taste of stout may be unusual, when combined with the the biscuity tart base and light chocolate soufflé the dish is remarkably satisfying.' *Ruth Lappin*

Serves 6

For the Sable Breton:

200g butter

120g sugar

320g flour

20g baking powder

20g (from approx. 1 egg) egg yolk

For the Stout Ice Cream:

375g cream

375g stout

112g brown sugar

180g (from approx. 8-9 eggs) egg
  yolk

18g trimoline

For the Chocolate 'Soufflé':

80g chocolate

40g butter

80g egg yolk

120g (from approx. 5-6 eggs) egg
  white

40g sugar

TO MAKE THE SABLE BRETON:

1 Cream the butter and sugar. Add the flour and baking powder, combine. Add egg yolk.

2 Rest in fridge, chill. Roll out. Rest again in fridge.

3 Cook at 180°C for 6 minutes.

TO MAKE THE STOUT ICE CREAM:

1 Boil the cream, stout and trimoline together.

2 Whisk the brown sugar and egg yolk together.

3 Pour half the boiling liquid over the egg and sugar. Mix thoroughly. Return to pan, bring the mix to 77°C.

4 Pass through a chinois, cool over ice, and churn.

TO MAKE THE CHOCOLATE 'SOUFFLÉ':

1. Melt the chocolate and butter together. Add the egg yolk to the chocolate mixture.

2. Whip egg whites, add sugar and whip to firm but not foamy peaks. Fold the egg white into the chocolate mix.

3. Pipe rounded domes into tart bases.

5 Bake at 180°C for 4 minutes.

TO SERVE:

Dust with cocoa.

Drinks

Oolong tea or Banyuls.

PAUL KELLY

Dark Chocolate & Catalan Crème Cake

'Over the years I have developed a respect for the flavours and presentation of Spanish pastry work. Catalan cream is a modern version of crème brulée, consisting of a burnt sugar crust with set custard underneath. Serve with a super light chocolate cream and a chewy hazelnut dacquoise for a very special cake.' *Paul Kelly*

Serves 8-10

For the Hazelnut Dacquoise:

1000g* egg whites

400g sugar

600g toasted hazelnuts

600g icing sugar

400g muscovado sugar

100g cake flour

2g sea salt

TO MAKE THE HAZELNUT DACQUOISE:

1 Combine and sift flour, hazelnut powder and icing sugar.

2 Whisk white sugar and salt to stiff peaks. Gently add sifted dry ingredients and finally add muscovado.

3 Pipe onto 60x40cm trays and sprinkle with icing sugar. Bake at 180°C for 25 minutes.

* Paul Kelly works his liquids, including egg whites, in weights.

For the Catalan Crème:

1250g cream

1250g milk

700g sugar

600g egg yolks

Pinch cinnamon

Lemon zest

For the Dark Chocolate Cream:

1160g cream

1540g dark chocolate (ideally 67% cocoa)

1540g cream, semi-whipped

To Garnish:

Chocolate leaf dust with copper powder

TO MAKE THE CATALAN CRÈME:

1 Put the cream, milk and half sugar into pot and boil.

2 Combine rest of sugar egg yolks in a bowl, slowly add boiled mix stirring all the time and finally add cinnamon and zest.

3 Place into mould and bake at 180°C for about 30 minutes.

4 Remove from oven, cool and freeze. Before assembly you must caramelise surface.

TO MAKE THE DARK CHOCOLATE CREAM:

1 Heat 1160g cream to 75°C and pour onto dark chocolate pistols, mix until smooth.

2 Allow to cool slightly before folding in semi-whipped cream to obtain a shiny, smooth chocolate cream.

FINAL ASSEMBLY:

1 Pour a layer of chocolate cream onto base of mould. Place your caramelised Catalan crème gently on top. Another layer of chocolate crème and finally hazelnut dacquoise.

2 Freeze.

3 Remove from mould and spray immediately for velvet effect. Garnish with chocolate leaf dust with copper powder.

Drinks

Banyuls, coffee, Madeira, or a Belgium Trappist Beer, such as Westmalle, from the Westmalle Brewery, or Coffee and Oatmeal Stout, from Dungarvan, Waterford.

Gooseberry & Elderflower Meringue Pie with Buttermilk Ice Cream

'A delicious summer dessert of seasonal elderflowers and gooseberries.' *Abigail Colleran*

Serves 8

For the Sweet Pastry:
500g butter
275g icing sugar
3 eggs
900g flour

For the Gooseberry Filling:
200g gooseberries, topped & tailed
50g sugar
150ml elderflower cordial
75g butter, unsalted, cubed
Cornflour, as required

For the Italian Meringue Topping:
250g egg whites
500g caster sugar

For the Buttermilk Ice Cream:
7 egg yolks
125g caster sugar
350ml cream
225ml buttermilk

TO MAKE THE SWEET PASTRY:

1 Cream butter and sugar together, incorporate the eggs. Add flour on a low speed and mix until just combined.

2 Wrap the pastry in cling film, chill in the fridge. Roll out and line a loose-bottomed 23-cm tart tin. Bake blind (see glossary) at 160°C for about 12-14 minutes, removing the weight for the last 5 minutes.

TO MAKE THE GOOSEBERRY FILLING:

1 Bring gooseberries, sugar and cordial to boil in a saucepan and reduce heat to a simmer.

2 Once the fruit has broken down to a pulp, stir in butter and thicken with cornflour until lightly set.

TO MAKE THE ITALIAN MERINGUE TOPPING:

Whisk whites and caster sugar over a bain-marie, bringing to 71°C. Remove from the heat and whisk on high speed until cold.

TO ASSEMBLE:

Spread the filling evenly in the tart shell. Pipe the meringue on top. Bake at 100°C for 12-15 minutes.

TO MAKE THE BUTTERMILK ICE CREAM:

1 Whisk the yolks and sugar together; scald the cream and whisk into the eggs and sugar.

2 Return to the heat. Stirring, bring to 76°C.

3 Chill over an ice bath. Whisk in the buttermilk. Churn to ice-cream consistency.

Drinks

Asti Spumante.

GEORGE SMITH

Homemade Spiced Apple Pie

'This gold-medal-winning recipe is best served with basil ice cream, seasonal berries and vanilla-flavoured custard.' *George Smith*

Serves 4

For the Pie:

500g flour

250g butter

125g sugar

3 eggs

4 apples

100g sugar

20g mixed spice

10g cornflour

2 tsp water

100g mixed seasonal berries

For the Custard and Ice Cream:

½ litre milk

3 egg yolks

60g sugar

1 vanilla pod

25g basil

TO MAKE THE PIE:

1 Mix flour, butter, sugar and eggs together in a bowl until combined.

2 Roll out and place in a mould.

3 Peel and slice apples and cook with sugar and mixed spice until hot.

4 Mix cornflour with water and add to hot apples to thicken.

5 Pour apple mixture into pastry mould and cover with pastry lid.

6 Bake for 20 minutes in a moderate oven.

TO MAKE THE CUSTARD AND ICE CREAM:

1 Boil milk and remove from heat.

2 Add egg yolks and sugar.

3 Place back on heat until mixture thickens.

4 Add vanilla pod seeds.

5 Take half of the custard mixture, add basil and place in the ice-cream machine until frozen.

TO SERVE:

Serve with the remaining custard and seasonal berries.

Drinks

Chilled glass of Sauternes or traditional teas and coffees.

Strawberry Macaroons with White Chocolate Ganache Filling

'This macaroon recipe includes a very rich white chocolate ganache filling. The smooth texture of the filling is complemented by the sweetness of the strawberry jam.' *John Clancy*

Makes 24

For the Macaroons:
500g ground almonds
500g icing sugar
160g egg white (7-8 eggs)
330g caster sugar
150g egg white
Red food colouring

For the White Chocolate Ganache:
300ml of fresh cream (35% fat)
500g good quality white chocolate, finely chopped
1 tsp of vanilla essence
100g strawberry jam

Chef's Tip
Filled macaroons can be successfully frozen. Allow 1 hour to defrost.

Drinks
Prosecco or a blond ale such as Smithwicks Blond Ale.

TO MAKE THE MACAROONS:

1 Pre-heat oven to 150°C.

2 Sieve together the almonds and icing sugar twice.

3 Boil the caster sugar to 118°C.

4 Whisk the 160g egg white, add the cooked sugar and make an Italian meringue.

5 Add the food colouring and add the almond mixture slowly.

6 With a spatula, fold in the 150g egg white to a dropping consistency.

7 Pipe onto parchment paper on a baking tray. Lightly tap the tray on a table before baking.

8 Bake the macaroons until crisp and a foot has formed at the base of each, about 15 minutes.

9 Remove from the oven, place on a wire rack to cool.

TO MAKE THE WHITE CHOCOLATE GANACHE:

1 Boil the cream and vanilla in a small saucepan and pour over the chocolate in a bowl and allow to melt.

2 Stir the ganache to a smooth consistency and shine.

3 Place the mixture in the fridge to set.

4 Remove from fridge and whisk until it is light and smooth.

5 To assemble the macroons: lightly spread a small amount of strawberry jam on one macaroon, and then pipe a bulb of ganache on top.

6 Press another macaroon on top until the filling spreads evenly. Repeat for the remaining macaroons.

JAMES SHERIDAN

Strawberries & Cream

'Strawberries and cream is an ever-popular summer dessert, most famously consumed at the Wimbledon tennis tournament. This recipe uses Irish Mist liqueur which gives a subtle but slightly luxurious flavour to the lightly whipped cream.' *James Sheridan*

Serves 4

400g of Irish strawberries
40g of caster sugar
500ml double cream
70ml Irish Mist liqueur
4 Martini-style glasses

1 Add the cream and sugar to a large bowl.
2 Beat the cream, being careful not to over-whip it.
3 Add the Irish Mist.
4 Add your strawberries to the cream (keep some for presentation).
5 Mix strawberries and cream until all strawberries are covered in the cream.
6 Place the mixture evenly into the martini glass.
7 Place a strawberry on top for presentation and serve.

Variation
This dish can be used with different berries such as raspberries, blackberries and blueberries, or a selection of mixed berries. An orange-flavoured liqueur like Grand Marnier or Cointreau, instead of Irish Mist, would also work well.

Drinks
Moscato d'Asti, Rosé Champagne; Muscat de Rivesalt wines or a Lambic fruit beer (with flavours such as Framboise or Strawberry), or Belgian Kriek Lambic Beers.

SHANNON DICKSON

Raspberry & Lemon Curd Pavlova with Toasted Almonds

'Pavlova is one of those desserts that is always on standby in my kitchen because it is very easy to make, versatile and a great way to finish a meal.' *Shannon Dickson*

Serves 8

For the Meringue:

120g egg whites (4 eggs: best at
  room temperature)
240g caster sugar
20g cornflour
1tbsp boiling water
1tsp white wine vinegar
1tsp vanilla essence

To Garnish:

1-2 punnet of fresh raspberries
100g toasted flaked almonds
250ml fresh whipped cream

For the Lemon Curd:

4 large egg yolks
1 large egg
3-4 lemons, zested
140g caster sugar
120ml lemon juice
215g unsalted butter, cut into cubes
Pinch of salt

TO MAKE THE LEMON CURD:

1 Whisk the yolks, whole egg, lemon zest and juice with the sugar in a saucepan on a low heat. Add the butter, a cube at a time, mixing until it is all incorporated.
2 Bring the mix to the boil, moving the mix across the pan so that it doesn't stick.
3 Once the mix coats the back of a wooden spoon, sieve and press through into a clean bowl, cover and cool before assembling.

TO MAKE THE MERINGUE BASE:

1 Set your oven to 140°C/120°C fan. Scald out your electric mixing bowl. Whisk all the meringue ingredients in the bowl for 8–10 minutes until glossy and thick.
2 Line a baking tray with silicone paper and draw a 20cm-round template on the paper.
3 Using a palette knife, spread the meringue in the circle.
4 Bake the pavlova for 60-75 minutes until the meringue is a light fawn colour.
5 Once baked, take out of the oven and cool. Pavlova can be kept in an airtight container for 3-4 days before filling.

TO ASSEMBLE:

Take the pavlova and turn it upside down on the serving plate. Spread the lemon curd over the meringue and top with freshly whipped cream, fresh raspberries and toasted flaked almonds.

ไ

Drinks

Sparkling white wine such as Moscato d'Asti, Rosé or demi-sec Champagne or a Belgian Kriek Lambic Beer.

MICHEL ROUX SNR

Soufflé au Chocolat

'These are heavenly; to make them even more divine, slip a spoonful of fresh, churned vanilla ice cream into the centre of each soufflé at the table.' *Michel Roux Snr*

Serves 4

For the Soufflé:

40g softened butter, to grease dishes

40g caster sugar, to coat dishes

15g cocoa powder, sifted

120g plain chocolate (70% cocoa solids), chopped in small pieces

10 medium egg whites

40g caster sugar

For the Pastry Cream:

350ml milk

80g caster sugar

4 medium egg yolks

30g plain flour

To finish:

Icing sugar, to dust

Drinks

Banyuls or a ruby port.

Butter 4 individual 10cm soufflé dishes and coat the insides with the sugar.

TO MAKE THE PASTRY CREAM:

1 Slowly bring the milk and two-thirds of the sugar to the boil in a small pan.

2 Whisk the egg yolks and remaining sugar to a ribbon consistency, then incorporate the flour.

3 Pour the hot milk on to the yolks, whisking continuously.

4 Return to the pan and whisk over a low heat for 1 minute.

5 Pour into a bowl, cover with cling film and let cool slightly.

6 Preheat the oven to 190°C and heat a baking sheet.

TO MAKE THE SOUFFLÉ:

1 Whisk cocoa powder and chopped chocolate into 280g of the pastry cream (keep the rest for another use).

2 Beat the egg whites to a thick foam, add 40g sugar and beat until they form soft peaks.

3 Fold one-third into the pastry cream using a whisk, then delicately fold in the rest with a large spoon; the mixture will be fairly loose.

4 Divide the mixture between the soufflé dishes, filling them to the top.

5 Stand on the hot baking sheet and cook for 10 minutes. Dust the tops with icing sugar, place on warm plates and serve immediately.

ROSS LEWIS

Spiced Tea-soaked Prune Sponge with a Stout Glaze & Lemon & Ginger Ice cream

'This recipe might appear very challenging to create but it is worth the effort.' Ross Lewis

Serves 8

For the Tea-soaked Prunes:
250ml water
100g caster sugar
2 Earl Grey tea bags
1 lemon, cut in slices
2 bay leaves
16 ready-to-eat Agen prunes

For the Mascarpone Mousse:
250g mascarpone
125ml milk
125ml cream
40g sugar
2.5g Hy-foamer
0.5g xantana

TO MAKE THE TEA-SOAKED PRUNES:
1 Boil the water and sugar for 2 minutes, add other ingredients and bring back to the boil.
2 Leave to soak for a minimum of 12 hours. De-stone prunes and cut roughly.

FOR THE MASCARPONE MOUSSE:
1 Place in a bowl and add 2 tablespoons of the cooking syrup and mix. Set aside.
2 Mix the sugar, xantana and Hy-foamer in a small bowl.
3 Mix the cream and milk in a bowl and with a small hand blender slowly blend in the sugar mixture, mixing for 2 minutes.
4 Put the mascarpone in a stand-up mixer with a jug attachment and blend with the milk cream mix, pass through a fine chinois and fill a Chantilly gun ¾ the way, add 1 gas cartridge and shake well; rest for 1 hour.

For the Tea & Lemon Sorbet:

125g sugar

125ml water

15g inverted sugar

3g super neutrose

½ lemon, sliced

5g ginger, sliced

1 bay leaf

2 Earl Grey tea bags

200ml sparkling water

For the Ginger Gel:

50g ginger, peeled & sliced

100g sugar

100g glucose

200g water

For the Clementine Compote:

2 clementines, washed & quartered

150g sugar

20g glucose

½ vanilla pod

300ml water

TO MAKE THE TEA AND LEMON SORBET:

1 Bring the sugar and water to the boil, add inverted sugar and super neutrose and boil for 1 minute.

2 Add lemon, ginger and the bay leaf and boil for another 1 minute. Take off the heat and add tea bags. Allow to cool to room temperature.

3 Add sparkling water and pass through a chinois. Freeze in Pacojet containers or churn in an ice-cream machine.

TO MAKE THE GINGER GEL:

1 Place the ingredients in a pot and bring to the boil and simmer for 3 hours.

2 Set up a thermo-mix and blend on full for 3 minutes.

3 Pass through a chinois and cool down.

TO MAKE THE CLEMENTINE COMPOTE:

1 Put the clementines in a pot, cover with water and bring to the boil and strain. Do this one more time and strain the liquid off. Add the sugar, water, glucose and the vanilla, bring to the boil and turn down to a low simmer for 12 hours.

2 Cool and keep the clementines in the liquid.

For the Muscovado & Ginger Biscuits:

35g butter

100g dark muscovado sugar

30g plain flour

60g egg whites

20g gingerbread powder

20g demerara sugar

FOR THE MUSCOVADO AND GINGER BISCUITS:

1 Melt butter in a pan, add the sugar and mix to a paste.

2 Remove from the heat and mix in the flour and egg whites.

3 Pass through a tamis or drum sieve into a clean bowl and leave to rest overnight in the fridge.

4 The next day, preheat the oven to 170°C.

5 Spread the biscuit mix on a Silpat (or non-stick baking mat), using a 2x4cm template, and sprinkle the gingerbread powder and demerara sugar over the top.

6 Bake for 9 minutes until crisp and golden brown. Transfer to a wire rack and leave to cool completely.

FINAL PRESENTATION:

In a shallow bowl, place 5 large soaked prunes, put a teaspoon of clementine compote in 3 random positions between the prunes and drizzle with ginger gel. Add a quenelle of tea and lemon sorbet on top and pipe a generous amount of mascarpone mousse from the Chantilly gun. Place 3 shards of ginger biscuit into the mousse and finish with orange powder.

Drinks

PX Sherry, tawny port, Auslese Riesling, coffee or a flavoured porter, such as Ginger Porter, from Rascal's Brewing Company, Dublin.

Drinks

PX Sherry, Tokaji, Sauternes, green tea or a Double Indian
pale ale, such as English Shepherd Neame IPA, Kent, or
Irish O'Hara's Double IPA.

KEELAN HIGGS

Treacle Tart & Star Anise Ice Cream

'Simple, luxurious and perfect for cold evenings by the fire. There is no treacle in this recipe, but the anise ice cream gives the treacly flavour and cuts through the sweetness of the tart. For a variation, use honey instead of golden syrup, or treacle for a very rich intense tart. It also works well with vanilla ice cream.' *Keelan Higgs*

Serves 8-10

For the Pastry:

250g butter

200g icing sugar

3 eggs

500g plain flour

For the Filling:

650g golden syrup

3 eggs

50g cream

200g ground almonds

100g fresh breadcrumbs

For the Anise Ice Cream:

35g star anise

625ml milk

125ml cream

100g caster sugar

6 egg yolks

TO MAKE THE PASTRY CASE:

1. Cream butter and sugar. Beat in eggs one by one, then mix in flour. Chill the pastry in the fridge for an hour, then roll out into pastry case.

2. Blind bake (see glossary) at 160°C for 30 minutes. Remove beans and bake for a further 20 minutes.

TO MAKE THE FILLING:

1 Preheat oven to 150°C.

2 Mix the golden syrup, eggs, cream and ground almonds until smooth. Add the breadcrumbs and mix to porridge-like consistency.

3 Cook for 35 minutes. Reduce temperature to 120°C and cook for a further 20 minutes, or until set.

TO MAKE THE ANISE ICE CREAM:

1 Place anise on a tray in the oven at 160°C for 2 minutes until toasted.

2 Cream sugar and egg yolks together in a bowl.

3 Bring milk and cream to the boil and pour over creamed egg and sugar mix.

4 Return all ingredients to heat and reduce heat to 85°C. Keep on the heat for 3 minutes.

5 Chill for 12 hours, then freeze.

PAULINE DANAHER

White & Dark Chocolate Mousse

'When making the white chocolate mousse the content of cream in the recipe needs to be reduced to 630ml. This mousse can be served in individual glasses and decorated with chocolate decorations or chocolate shavings. Make the dark chocolate mousse first as this sets quickly.' *Pauline Danaher*

Serves 10-12

For Dark Chocolate Mousse:
508g dark chocolate buttons
850ml cream
100g honey
6 egg yolks
4 whole eggs

For White Chocolate Mousse:
508g white chocolate buttons
850ml cream
100g honey
6 egg yolks
4 whole eggs

1 Boil the honey in a pot. Place the eggs and the egg yolks in a large bowl over a low heat and whisk. Slowly add the boiled honey to the eggs, continuing to whisk. Gradually increase the heat so the eggs and honey emulsify. This can take up to 10 minutes. Do not allow the temperature to rise above 65°C.

2 Place the dark chocolate in a bowl over a pot of hot water and melt the chocolate slowly.

3 Whisk the cream to soft peaks and refrigerate.

4 Fold the eggs and honey into the melted chocolate while warm and mix well.

5 Fold in the cream to the cool mixture of chocolate and eggs (this needs to be cool, otherwise the mixture will separate).

6 Pour into glasses, only half filling, and place in fridge. Make the white chocolate mousse using the same process as above but with less cream. Leave to set in the fridge.

7 Finish with chocolate decorations just before serving or dust with chocolate shavings.

Drinks
Coffee, port, Banyuls, stout or a barley wine beer, such as Gallows Hill Barley Wine, Dungarvan Brewing Company.

Rye Bread & Beer Ice Cream with Caramelised White Chocolate Mousse & Apple Root

'The integrated flavours of this dish are inspired by the organic and local produce of Gent, Belgium.' Rose Greene

Serves 4-6

For the Ice Cream:

500g milk

250g cream

200g rye bread (pieces)

150g brown sugar

100g egg yolks

250g dark beer (Rodenbach)

For the Mousse:

250g caramelised white chocolate

200g buttermilk

50g sour cream

1 leaf gelatine

200g lightly whipped cream

For the Crumbs:

Dried crumbs from making the ice cream

125g crumbs

12g sugar

12g butter

TO MAKE THE ICE CREAM:

1 Bring milk and cream to the boil, add rye pieces, and bring back to the boil.

2 Whisk yolks and brown sugar together, add ¼ of the milk/cream mix and then combine all together.

3 Cook out like a normal crème anglaise to 82°C. Finish by adding beer and passing through a sieve (reserving rye bread), chill and churn custard into ice cream. Dry the rye bread and use for toasting.

TO MAKE THE MOUSSE:

1 Melt the caramelised white chocolate with half the buttermilk (do not overheat as it could split).

2 Dissolve the gelatine with the rest of the buttermilk and mix with the chocolate mix.

3 Whisk together chocolate mix, the rest of the buttermilk and the sour cream, cool slightly over ice and fold in whipped cream.

4 Place in an iSi canister and charge with 1 gas charge. Store in the fridge.

FOR THE CRUMBS:

Melt sugar and butter, coat the crumbs, toast until golden at 140°C, let cool, blitz and pass through a sieve into a fine powder.

For the Apple Root:

1 small apple root/yacon

1 bottle of Rodenbach vintage beer

FOR THE APPLE ROOT:

Slice apple root thinly with a mandolin and soak in Rodenbach beer for a few hours.

TO SERVE:

Serve a quenelle of rye bread ice cream on the base of the bowl, cover with the white chocolate mousse, and sprinkle with rye crumbs

Drinks

Muscat Beaumes de Venise wine or Imperial Stout.

Chef's Tip

For the caramelised white chocolate: place white chocolate on a tray and put into an oven at 120°C. Stir and turn every 10 minutes, giving a really nice dark brown colour (may take up to 1 hour). If the chocolate dries out, a little cocoa butter can be added.

RYE BREAD & BEER ICE CREAM WITH CARAMELISED WHITE CHOCOLATE MOUSSE & APPLE ROOT 145

BREADS & BAKING

Dough Making - techniques

PREPARATION

1. All ingredients should be weighed in advance and be at ambient temperature except for the water or milk.
2. These liquids need to be at a specific temperature to achieve the correct dough temperature (see Baker's Tip).
3. If you are using a lidded machine the increase in dough temperature will be higher during mixing.
4. To achieve professional standards, liquids should be weighed, not measured. 1ml of water weighs 1g. To accommodate the home chef many of the recipes in this book use mls.

MIXING

1. The dough may be mixed by hand or in a machine with a dough hook.
2. Place the liquids and the crumbed yeast into the bowl first then the flour and then any other ingredients.
3. Mix by hand or with a spatula until all of the flour has been wetted and there are visible signs of gluten formation, takes about 2 to 3 minutes. On a machine this will take 1 to 2 minutes on the slowest speed.

KNEADING

On a machine this takes 5 to 7 minutes on speed 1.

Dough making, step 1.

Dough making, step 2.

KNEADING BY HAND

1 By hand, empty the contents of the bowl onto a clean dry surface, not marble or granite.

2 Begin by stretching the dough out in front of you with the heel of your hand, pushing it down and away from you so as you are developing the gluten structure.

Dough making, step 3.

3 Press and stretch the dough from the farthest part away from you, slowly working back towards the nearest part of the dough to you.

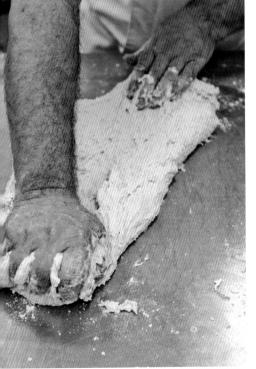

Dough making, step 4.

4 Turn the dough in a different direction and repeat. It will tear and stick for about 2 to 3 minutes until the gluten starts to develop. Continue kneading for a total of 9 to 10 minutes until the dough feels smooth and elastic.

Baker's Tip

To achieve the correct water temperature and the correct dough temperature of 28°C, the following is traditionally used: 2 x dough temperature minus the flour temperature equals the water temperature.

Dough making, step 5.

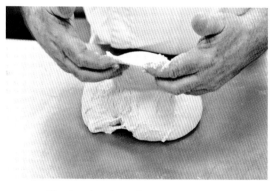

Testing for the 'gluten window'.

5 Form it into a ball shape and place into a bowl large enough for it to more than double in size and cover loosely with plastic so the dough does not skin.

Variation

The French method of kneading is for high hydration doughs or very soft, rich doughs. Hold the side of the dough closest to you between your thumb and fingers, lift it up until it has stretched as far as it will go and flip it forward in a fluid motion to fold the dough over onto itself, slapping on the bench in front of you.

Rotate the dough slightly, tucking in the edges and repeat until the dough is fully developed, about 10 minutes until the dough stretches easily and has become very smooth and elastic

GLUTEN/DOUGH DEVELOPMENT

To check if a white bread dough is fully developed, gently stretch the dough between your hands until you can see through a thin film of dough – the 'gluten window'.

FERMENTATION TIME

The bulk fermentation time is the time between the finished dough and the time the dough is scaled. This includes any knock-backs, stretches or folds.

KNOCK-BACK/STRETCH AND FOLD

This is to expel gases from the dough, put the yeast in contact with new food sources, equalise the dough temperature and add strength and stability to the gluten network. The stretch and fold technique is usually for wetter doughs. It is a more gentle form of knocking back and can be used for all doughs.

SCALING AND FIRST MOULDING

The dough is portioned into appropriate weights and formed into, usually, a tight ball shape.

INTERMEDIATE PROOF

The dough is rested before it is formed into its final shape.

PROOF

The final proof is where the dough is left to reach its full volume. The dough should be lightly dusted and loosely covered with a piece of plastic to prevent skinning and still allow the dough to expand, unless it has been egg washed.

BAKING

Place in a pre-heated oven at the required temperature for the required time as per the recipe.

COOLING

After baking place on a cooling wire to cool.

 For an online demonstration of Robert's dough making and plaiting, scan the code.

DARINA ALLEN

Ballymaloe Brown Yeast Bread

'This highly nutritious bread is a Ballymaloe House favourite. White or brown sugar, honey, golden syrup, treacle, molasses or different flours may be used, to give slightly different flavours and textures. At Ballymaloe we use treacle with stone-ground wholemeal.' *Darina Allen*

Makes 1 loaf

400g strong (stone-ground) wholemeal flour plus 50g strong white flour

425ml water at blood heat

1 tsp black treacle or molasses

1 tsp salt

20-30g fresh, non-GM yeast

Sesame seeds, optional

Sunflower oil

1 Preheat the oven to 230°C.

2 The ingredients should all be at room temperature. Mix the flour with the salt. In a small bowl or Pyrex jug, mix the treacle with 150ml water, and crumble in the yeast.

3 Sit the bowl in a warm place to allow the yeast to start to work. After about 4 or 5 minutes it will have a creamy and slightly frothy appearance on top.

4 When ready, stir and pour it, with all the remaining water (275ml), into the flour to make a loose-wet dough. The mixture should be too wet to knead. Allow to sit for 7-10 minutes (time dependent on room temperature).

5 Brush the base and sides of a 13x20cm loaf tin with sunflower oil. Scoop the mixture into the greased tin. Sprinkle the top of the loaves with sesame seeds, if using. Put the tin in a warm place, close to the cooker or near a radiator. Cover with a tea towel to prevent a skin forming.

6 Just as the bread comes to the top of the tin, remove the tea towel and pop in the oven at 230°C for 20 minutes. Turn the oven down to 200°C for another 40-50 minutes, or until it looks nicely browned and sounds hollow when tapped. The bread will rise a little further in the oven. This is called 'oven spring'. If, however, the bread rises to the top of the tin before it goes into the oven it will continue to rise and flow over the edges.

7 Remove the loaf from the tin about 10 minutes before the end of cooking and put back into the oven to crisp all round; if you like a softer crust there is no need to do this.

Baker's Tip

Yeast is a living organism, requiring warmth, moisture and nourishment. Heat of over 50°C will kill yeast. The dough rises more rapidly with 30g yeast than with 25g yeast. Have the ingredients and equipment at blood heat. Dried yeast may be used. Follow the same method but use only half the weight given for fresh yeast. Allow longer to rise. Fast-acting yeast may also be used.

Variations:

You may also use 400g strong stone-ground wholemeal plus 50g rye or 450g strong (stone-ground) wholemeal flour. The quantity of water may need to be altered to achieve a dough that is just too wet to knead – in fact it does not require kneading.

Party Bread

'A lovely table decoration that can be eaten with soup, paté or any meal.' *Robert Humphries*

Makes 1 loaf (recipe can be halved to fit a 20cm tin, making 8 x 50g rounds, having one surrounded by 7)

500g strong flour

10g salt

60g soft butter

15g caster sugar

120g water

100g milk

50g egg

20g yeast, dried yeast (but not fast-acting yeast) may be used at half the quantity of fresh yeast

1 Bring the water and milk to the correct temperature (see Baker's Tip, p149).

2 Disperse the yeast and the caster sugar in the water and milk mixture.

3 Add the flour, salt, butter and the egg to the liquid and mix to a well-developed dough.

4 Dough temperature: 26°C.

5 Fermentation time: 60 minutes. Knock back after 45 minutes.

6 Scaling weight: 19 pieces at 45g.

7 Form into a ball shape.

8 Intermediate proof: 10 minutes. Keep covered.

9 Final mould round, egg wash and dip in alternate seeds, poppy, linseed, sunflower, sesame, to top as desired.

10 Place in a papered or greased 25cm loose-bottomed tin. Start with one in the centre, surrounded by six in the middle ring and an outer ring of twelve.

11 Proof time: 45 minutes.

12 Baking temperature: 210°C.

13 Baking time: 30 minutes.

Plaited Breads

'A decorative bread which can be eaten throughout the day and served with any topping you wish.'
Robert Humphries

Yields 4 x 500g plaits (can be halved or quartered)

For Batter Sponge:

500g baker's flour

500ml water

33g sugar

33g yeast, dried yeast (but not fast-
acting yeast) may be used at half
the quantity of fresh yeast

Dough Ingredients:

1066g batter sponge

750g baker's flour

60g milk powder

24g salt

85g butter

30ml water

150g eggs

TO MAKE THE BATTER SPONGE:

1 Disperse the yeast and sugar in the water, add the flour.

2 Mix together to form a batter and cover.

3 Set aside for 30 minutes.

TO MAKE THE DOUGH:

1 Mix all dough ingredients to a well-developed dough.

2 Dough temperature: 26°C.

3 Fermentation time: 10 minutes.

4 Scaling weight: 500g each plait.

5 Divide: 10 x 100g and 12 x 85g and first mould round.

6 Intermediate proof: 5 minutes. Keep covered.

TO SHAPE:

1 For the final mould shape, each strand to be 30 cm-long with tapered ends.

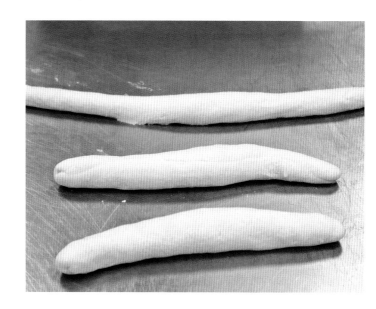

2 Lay the strands out in a fan with the tops touching, join and follow the plaiting sequence.

3 For a 5-string: 2 over 3, 5 over 2, 1 over 3, and repeat.

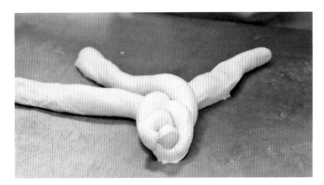

For a step-by-step demonstration scan the QR code on p151.

TO FINISH:

1 Egg-wash and place on silicone-papered tray.

2 Final proof time: 35 minutes at 28°C.

3 Re-egg wash and add seeds, if desired.

4 Baking temperature: 210°C.

5 Baking time: 25–30 minutes.

ROBERT HUMPHRIES

Potato & Dill Bread

'This bread is ideal for sandwiches, or served with soup or any meal.' *Robert Humphries*

Yields 2 x 500g breads (may be halved)

For the Starter:

150g strong flour

100g water

2g yeast, dried yeast (but not fast-acting yeast) may be used at half the quantity of fresh yeast

For the Dough:

240g starter

290g water

450g strong flour

12g salt

1g cracked black pepper

14g yeast, dried yeast (but not fast-acting yeast) may be used at half the quantity of fresh yeast

Added Ingredients:

200g baked potatoes, mashed

15g olive oil

7g fresh dill, chopped

To Press Out:

Maize grits

FOR THE STARTER:

1 Disperse the yeast in the water in a bowl, add the flour and mix to a dough. Cover with cling film.

2 Rest for 1 hour and place in fridge at 2-4°C overnight. Make sure the bowl is big enough as it will double in size.

TO MAKE THE DOUGH:

1 Mix all the dough ingredients to a very well-developed dough.

2 Add potato, olive oil, 7g fresh dill and mix well.

3 Dough temperature: 24°C.

4 Fermentation time: 60 minutes. Stretch and fold at 20 and 40 minutes.

5 Scaling weight: 3 Pieces at 400g. Hand up into a ball shape, on maize grits.

6 Intermediate proof: 15 minutes. Keep covered.

7 Press out in maize grits to a 20-cm disk. Place on linen cloths and cover.

8 Proof temp: 28°C.

9 Proof time: 60 minutes.

10 Lift carefully onto a tray, cut shamrock shape, or as desired, and rest for 5 minutes before baking. Spray with water and transfer to an oven.

11 Baking temperature: Load at 220°C and drop to 200°C.

12 Baking time: 30-35 minutes.

JAMES GRIFFIN

Seaweed Soda Bread

'By adding seaweed, rich in minerals and iodine, this recipe offers an Atlantic twist on a nation's favourite. Mixing by hand produces the bread's characteristic delicate crumb. The alginates in the seaweed also help to keep the bread fresher for longer.' *James Griffin*

Makes 3 x 550g loaves

350g 100% wholemeal flour
200g cake or pastry flour
50g wheat germ
5g salt
8g baking powder
8g bread soda
15g vegetable oil
15g seaweed powder (Noribake
  is readily available)
810g buttermilk

1 Set the oven to 225°C.
2 Sieve the cake flour, the bread soda and the baking powder together into a large bowl.
3 Blend the rest of the dry ingredients by hand, the wholemeal flour, seaweed powder, salt and wheat germ with the sieved ingredients.
4 Add the vegetable oil to the buttermilk and pour into the bowl. Gently mix, using an open hand for 30-40 seconds until it comes together.
5 Weigh the mix at 550g into rectangular 450g bread tins.
6 Cut the top with a knife and allow to stand for 15 minutes before placing in the oven.
7 Sprinkle some seeds or corn chips if required.
8 Bake at 225°C for 45 – 50 minutes until a hollow sound when base is tapped.
9 Allow to cool on a wire tray.

Baker's Tip
Delicious when served with butter, especially toasted, this bread also complements seafood canapés and will keep for several days when placed in a sealed plastic bag.

Carrot Cake

'This carrot cake is easy to prepare. It can be finished with a cream cheese topping but is equally nice just dusted with icing sugar.' *Pauline Danaher*

Serves 10-12

8 eggs

360ml vegetable oil

795g caster sugar

5g salt

500g strong flour

15g ground cinnamon

6g baking soda

2g baking powder

900g peeled carrots, grated

120g walnuts, roughly chopped

Cream Cheese Topping:

300g cream cheese

90g soft unsalted butter

½ tsp vanilla essence

175g icing sugar

1 Whisk the eggs until they are frothy on a medium speed. Turn the mixing machine down to a low speed and add the caster sugar and salt. Continue whisking until the sugar has been well incorporated.

2 Sieve all dry ingredients together. Remove the eggs and sugar from the mixing machine and fold in the dry ingredients, carrots and walnuts.

3 Place the mixture into a floured baking tray or ring and bake at 190°C for 50 minutes. To check if cooked, insert a skewer into the centre of the cake and remove. If it is clean the cake is ready.

4 Turn upside down in the cooking vessel and leave to cool.

5 Dust with icing sugar or add cream cheese topping.

TO MAKE THE CREAM CHEESE TOPPING:

1 Using a beater on the mixer, soften the cream cheese and then gradually add the butter. Mix well together.

2 Add the vanilla essence and icing sugar and mix until spreadable.

3 Spread on top of cooled carrot cake.

Chocolate & Cream Cheese Muffins

'A wonderfully moist muffin suited to a leisurely breakfast or brunch and easily created at home.'

Denise Connaughton

Serves 10

130g cream flour

5g baking powder

1.25g bread soda

1.25g salt

25g cocoa powder
 (70% cocoa solids)

85g caster sugar

125g whole egg

2.5ml vanilla essence

45g vegetable oil

Cream Cheese Filling:

50g cream cheese

25g caster sugar

Preheat oven to 200°C.

TO MAKE THE CREAM CHEESE FILLING:

Beat the cream cheese and caster sugar until smooth.

TO MAKE THE MUFFINS:

1 Sieve the cream flour, baking powder, bread soda, salt and cocoa powder into a bowl.

2 Add the caster sugar, mix through.

3 Add the egg, milk, vanilla essence and vegetable oil and mix until combined.

4 Spoon a small amount of the base muffin mix into each muffin case.

5 Drop a teaspoon of cream cheese mixture into the centre.

6 Spoon a small amount of the base muffin mix on top of the cream cheese to enclose it.

7 Bake for 20-25 minutes until set.

Variation

Double chocolate chip muffins: just add 75g of chocolate chips to the final stage of mixing at step 4 and omit the cream cheese.

CHOCOLATE & CREAM CHEESE MUFFINS 165

SHEONA FOLEY

Gluten-free Nutty Chocolate Torte

'This recipe is reminiscent of the wonderful Torta Caprese from the Italian island of Capri. A tale goes that this delicious cake came about by accident when the baker forgot to add the flour or perhaps mistook some cocoa for the flour. The result is a delicious chocolate and nut torte, bursting with crunchy nuts and dark chocolate, which is naturally gluten free.' *Sheona Foley*

Serves 10-12

200g unsalted butter

200g whole blanched almonds

50g walnuts or hazelnuts

200g dark chocolate
 (70% cocoa solids)

200g eggs

170g caster sugar

1tsp almond extract

1tsp coffee extract

Pinch of salt

Icing sugar (to serve)

1 Preheat the oven to 170°C.

2 Line the base of circular, 24cm-diameter cake tin with baking parchment.

3 Melt the butter and allow to cool.

4 Finely chop the dark chocolate and nuts in a food processor.

5 Separate the eggs.

6 Whisk the egg yolks together with the caster sugar until you reach the ribbon stage (see Baker's Tip below).

7 Gently fold the ground chocolate and nuts together with butter into the egg yolk/sugar mixture.

8 In a separate bowl with cleaned whisks, whisk the egg whites with a pinch of salt until they just hold stiff peaks. Add a quarter of this into the almond mixture to loosen. Fold in the remaining egg white gently.

9 Spread the mixture into the prepared cake tin.

10 Bake in a pre-heated oven for 55-60 minutes until firm.

11 Remove from oven and allow to cool in the tin.

12 Remove from tin and dust with icing sugar before serving.

Baker's Tip

The ribbon stage is achieved when the sugar is dissolved and the mixture thickens and becomes a pale yellow colour. If the whisks are lifted out above the mixture, they leave behind a trail or ribbon.

Oxford Lunch

'A popular, light fruit cake with the classic flaked almond top that can be enjoyed at any time. The method used here is the "Flour Batter Method" which produces a superior textured cake with longer keeping qualities and eliminates the risk of curdling.' *Ann-Marie Dunne*

Serves 12-14

150g or 3 eggs

150g caster sugar

1.25ml or ¼ tsp vanilla essence

1.25ml or ¼ tsp almond essence

150g butter

25g ground almonds

225g plain flour

10ml or 2 tsp glycerine

2.5 g or ½ tsp baking powder

40ml milk

280g sultanas

130g cherries halved

70g mixed peel

30g flaked almonds

1 Pre-heat the oven to 160°C.

2 Whisk eggs, sugar and essence until thick and light. Transfer to separate bowl and set aside.

3 Cream 170g of the flour, glycerine, ground almonds and butter until light using a beater and scrape down the bowl.

4 Add back in sponged egg and sugar mixture in 3 to 4 additions on a slow speed, scraping down the sides of the bowl between each addition.

5 Fold in remainder flour and baking powder.

6 Add milk and mix gently.

7 Fold in fruit gently and mix evenly through cake mixture.

8 Place the mixture into a lined 1 kg loaf tin or a 20cm cake tin.

9 Flatten top with wet hand, sprinkle with flaked almonds, and bake for approximately 1¾-2 hours.

10 Test with skewer to check if baked. It should come out clean when placed into the centre of the cake.

11 When cool, the cake should be wrapped to keep it fresh longer.

Baker's Tip

Wash dried fruit before use, to clean and rehydrate. This results in a superior product with longer keeping qualities. Wash dried fruits in a sieve under warm running water until the water runs clear; finally rinse in cold water. Place onto tea towels overnight to dry out. The washed fruit can be stored in a cool place in containers, but use within 1 month.

Sour Cherry & Pistachio Brownies

'This is a favourite tried and trusted brownie recipe which you will enjoy making – and eating – over and over.'
Darrren Harris

Serves 12

For the Brownies:

208g soft brown dark sugar

208g caster sugar

188g soft flour (not self-raising, as a dense texture is desired)

7 large eggs

170g unsalted butter

170g salted butter

340g dark chocolate (high quality)

200g unsalted whole pistachios

200g semi-candied sour cherries

Chocolate Ganache for Finishing/ Plate Decoration:

200g single cream

200g dark chocolate (high quality)

TO MAKE THE BROWNIES:

1 Line a brownie tray (23x30cm) with non-stick paper.

2 Rub flour into sugar to ensure a smooth flour-sugar mix with no lumps.

3 Break up the eggs lightly, but do not whisk.

4 Warm up chocolate and butter until liquid.

5 Add chocolate-butter mix to eggs and mix well.

6 Add this to the sugar-flour mix, making sure there are no lumps. Gently swirl around until almost combined.

7 Finally, gently swirl in pistachios and cherries.

8 Ensure brownie batter is smooth, tip into tray, level out, and bake at 165°C for about 18 minutes.

9 When presenting or cooling, invert the brownies: present smooth side up.

TO MAKE THE CHOCOLATE GANACHE:

Gently melt the chocolate and cream together in a pot.

TO SERVE:

Either pour the ganache over the top of the cooling inverted brownies, smooth out and set, or serve the brownies slightly warm with warm ganache on the side, and raspberries and vanilla ice cream.

Variations

If the sour cherries are unavailable use firm, fresh pitted cherries or good quality cherries from a can in syrup. If using salted pistachios, rinse well in water and pat dry.

ANN-MARIE DUNNE

Tea Brack

'Unlike the traditional Irish barmbrack, traditionally made for Halloween, using a fermented sweet dough, this tea brack falls into the tea-cake category. It is a delicious, moist cake that is low in fat and can be enjoyed at any time, especially with a cup of tea or coffee.' *Ann-Marie Dunne*

Serves 12-14

200g sultanas

200g raisins

50g mixed peel

50g cherries

225ml cold, strong tea

125g brown sugar

50g or 1 egg

30g chopped walnuts

250g cream flour

10g or 2 level tsp baking powder

5g or 1 level tsp mixed spices

50g melted butter

35ml milk

1 Soak fruit, cherries, mixed peel, sugar and cold tea for 45 minutes or overnight.

2 Pre-heat the oven to 170°C (fan). Sieve flour baking powder and spices together in a large mixing bowl.

3 Add egg, walnuts and melted butter to soaked fruit mix and stir well.

4 Add fruit mixture to dry ingredients and mix thoroughly.

5 Fold in milk.

6 Place into a lined 1kg loaf tin.

7 Flatten top with a wet hand and bake for 60-65 minutes.

Baker's Tip

See Baker's Tip for dried fruit from the Oxford Lunch recipe.

ANN-MARIE DUNNE

Sticky Ginger Cake

'Originally from the sugar-and-spice island of Jamaica, this cake is dark, sticky, and fragrant with ginger, a warm welcome at any time, especially when spread with butter.' *Ann-Marie Dunne*

Serves 12-14

100g or 2 eggs

120g caster sugar

120g butter

120g treacle

120g golden syrup

150ml fresh milk

280g strong flour

1 tsp bread soda

1 tsp ground ginger

2 tsp mixed spice

75g crystallised ginger,
   chopped (optional)

4 crushed sugar cubes

1 Whisk eggs and sugar until light and fluffy.

2 Heat butter, treacle and golden syrup together until butter is melted; do not boil.

3 Whisk hot mixture into egg mixture and add milk and whisk.

4 Sieve flour, spices, and bread soda together. Fold into egg mixture and beat until lump free.

5 Add in chopped crystallised ginger, if using, at end.

6 Pour into lined 1kg loaf tin.

7 Sprinkle with crushed sugar cubes.

8 When baked, cool, wrap and store for 24 hours before eating.

Baker's Tip

When using syrup, place tin in a pan of hot water for a few minutes before measuring; this makes it easier to use.

COCKTAILS TO SUIT THE OCCASION

Cocktail recipes are constantly evolving as new products, methods, modern technology and cocktail-training drive the creative process; they are created to suit specific dining experiences or celebrations. These mixed drinks may be shaken, stirred, blended, muddled or built, depending upon the ingredients, or the texture or flavour required. The cocktail recipes here appeal across the seasons, times of the day and courses of a meal; they are divided into five categories: pre-dinner, all-day, after-dinner cocktail, shooters and alcohol-free cocktails.

The cocktail recipes in these pages are based on service for one person.

COCKTAILS

Left: Claire Gaffney, BSc, Bar Studies Graduate, winner of the Second Irish Distillers Cocktail Competition, 2006.

Pre-dinner Cocktails

These are short-drink cocktails of an aperitif type served before lunch, dinner or early in the evening. The taste and quality is usually dry to medium dry.

AMERICANO

Created at Gaspare Campari's Bar, Milan, Italy, in 1861, this refreshing cocktail was originally known as the Milano-Torino (from the two ingredients – Campari from Milan and Cinzano from Turin). The name changed to the Americano when it was made popular by American tourists visiting Italy during the prohibition era.

3cl sweet vermouth, 3cl Campari bitter, soda water

1 Stir the ingredients (not soda water) together gently in an old-fashioned, low-ball glass with fresh ice cubes.
2 Top up with soda water.
3 Garnish with half slice of orange.

OYSTER PEARL

This simple and very elegant cocktail was created by Con McCullagh, Slattery's Lounge, Long Mile Road, Dublin, winning bronze for Ireland at the World Cocktail Competition in Los Angeles, USA, in 1973.

2cl Gilbey's Gin, 2cl Cinzano Bianco vermouth, 2cl Tio Pepe (dry sherry)

1 Pour all ingredients into a mixing glass with ice and stir (3 minutes minimum).
2 Strain the contents into a small chilled martini cocktail glass.
3 Garnish with lemon zest and a lemon twist.

LA FLORIDITA DAIQUIRI

This recipe is from the 1934 *Bar La Florida Cocktails* guide, and was created in Floridita Bar, Havana, Cuba by Constante Ribalaigua. El Floridita Daiquiri, with maraschino liqueur, is a variation on the classic daiquiri.

6cl Cuban rum, juice of half fresh lime, 1 tsp white sugar or sugar syrup (increase if too tart), 1 tsp maraschino (cherry) liqueur

1 Blend all ingredients with crushed ice until smooth.
2 Pour un-strained into a coupette or large martini glass.
3 Garnish with a fresh lime shell and maraschino (red) cherry.

Oyster Pearl.

La Floridita Daiquiri.

HIGHLAND SAPPHIRE

Inspired by the classic pre-dinner sour cocktails of the US prohibition, this cocktail was created by lecturer James Murphy in 2003 for the 29th World Cocktail Competition. A balance of spice, sour and sweet flavours delivers a perfect pre-dinner cocktail.

1.5cl Drambuie liqueur, 4cl Bombay Sapphire gin, 2cl fresh lemon juice, 0.5cl egg white, 0.5cl Monin Green Banana syrup

1 Add all the ingredients (except syrup) to a cocktail shaker with ice, shake briskly for 2-3 minutes. Strain into a chilled martini cocktail glass and add the Green Banana Syrup last.
2 Garnish with a full slice of lime (cut in a wheel design), fan of (narrowly cut) pineapple leaves and one pearl onion.

LUXURY MINUTE

A perfectly balanced, classic aperitif drink for the modern-day cocktail drinker, created by advanced cocktail studies DIT student Guido Martino, Portmarnock Hotel and Golf Links, County Dublin in 2009.

2.5cl Chopin Potato Vodka, 1.5cl Cointreau, 1.25cl sweet vermouth, 1.25cl dry vermouth, 0.5cl Scotch whisky, dash Angostura bitters.

1 Pour all the ingredients into a mixing glass with ice and stir briskly.
2 Strain into a chilled Martini glass.
3 Garnish with fennel stem, salmon tartare and microleaves.

BITTER BEG

This cocktail was created by DIT bar studies graduate Victor Petrakov, Saba Restaurant, Dublin for the Beam Cocktail Challenge in 2013.

3.5cl Kilbeggan Irish whiskey, 2 dashes Fee Brothers Cranberry Bitters, 3cl blackcurrant and vanilla tea sugar syrup, 1cl lemon juice.

1 Add all ingredients to a cocktail shaker and shake with ice.
2 Double (or fine) strain into a chilled Champagne flute glass.
3 Garnish with lemon twist and fresh blackcurrants.

Highland Sapphire.

Bitter Beg.

All-day Cocktails

Long-drink cocktails can be served throughout the day and night. The taste and quality is medium to neutral in flavour.

ANGEL FRUIT

Full of tasty flavours, this recipe was created by Deirdre Byrne, Mint Bar, Westin Hotel, Dublin, winning a Gold medal (Fancy Drink Section) at the World Cocktail Competition in 2013.

4cl Bombay Sapphire gin, 1.5cl Villa Massa Limoncello, 1.5cl Martini Bianco, 3cl Finest Call Raspberry Purée, 4cl Caraïbos Pure Fruit Juice Apple, 1.5cl fresh lemon juice

1 Add all the ingredients to a cocktail shaker with ice, shake hard.
2 Strain the contents into an old-fashioned glass and add some ice.
3 Garnish with shaped cuts (using a pastry cutter) of apple, lime and butternut squash all skewered together with a fresh raspberry.

BLUE MOON

Perfect for long days in the sun, this tropical long-drink cocktail was created by legendary bartender Johnny Johnston, Standard Telephone Social Club, Newtownabbey, County Antrim, winning Ireland's first overall gold medal at the World Cocktail Competition in Portugal, 1982.

3.5cl gin, 1.75cl Blue Curacao liqueur, 1.75cl Cointreau liqueur, 7cl pineapple juice, 7cl Schweppes tonic water

1 Add all the ingredients to a cocktail shaker with ice (except the tonic water), shake hard.
2 Strain into a tall glass with ice and top with tonic water.
3 Garnish with pineapple wedge, green cherry and straws.

FULL OF PASSION

DIT bar studies graduate Claire Gaffney created this winner for the Sixth Irish Distillers Cocktail Competition, 2010.

4cl Absolut Vanilia, 2.5cl ginger & lemongrass cordial, 2.5cl passion fruit liqueur, 5cl apple juice, half stick of lemon grass

1 Add all the ingredients to a cocktail shaker and muddle first then shake the contents briskly with ice.
2 Strain into a tall glass with cubed ice and a little crushed ice on top.
3 Garnish with slices of fresh apple and straws.

Above: Deirdre Byrne prepares her gold-medal-winning cocktail 'Angel Fruit' in Prague, Czech Republic, 2013.
Bottom left: Blue Moon.
Bottom right: Full of Passion.

Autumn Sensation.

Morning Dew.

Life's A Peach.

AUTUMN SENSATION

A refreshing mix which balances spice, sweetness and freshness, this cocktail was created by DIT graduate and current General Manager of Bijou Bistro, Rathgar, Martin Meade for the 2011 Irish final of the Bacardí legacy competition. Be careful if you attempt to flame the orange oils.

50cl Bacardí, 8-year-old

30cl Martini Rosso

25cl fresh orange juice

15cl fresh lemon juice

1 bar spoon of sweet Spanish red pepper

1 bar spoon peach purée

2 dash orange bitters

1 Chill your cocktail shaker and cocktail glass.

2 Muddle the sweet Spanish peppers and the peach purée together in a dry cocktail shaker. Add the rum, martini, fruit juices and orange bitters and dry shake.

3 Add ingredients into your chilled shaker and shake vigorously.

4 Double-strain into a chilled cocktail glass.

5 Garnish with micro coriander herbs. Flame the oils of a fresh orange skin over your drink.

MORNING DEW

A perfect party cocktail, created by John McLoughlin, Dubliner Bar, Jurys Hotel, Ballsbridge, winning the 1982 European Cocktail Championship, Cannes, France.

4cl Tullamore Dew Irish whiskey, 2cl Crème de Bananes liqueur, 1.5cl Blue Curacao liqueur, 12cl grapefruit juice, fresh cream.

1 Add all ingredients (except cream) to a cocktail shaker with ice and shake.

2 Strain into a highball (tall) glass with ice.

3 Garnish with orange twist, red cherry and straws, float fresh cream on top.

LIFE'S A PEACH

DIT bar studies graduate Ian Alvey, BrewTonic Enterprise, Dublin, won the 2009 Fifth Irish Distillers Cocktail Competition with this tropical treat.

6cl Absolut Peach vodka, 2cl passion fruit syrup, 8cl cranberry juice, 1.5cl lime juice

1 Add all the ingredients to a cocktail shaker with ice, shake briskly.

2 Strain into a Hurricane glass and add some cubed and crushed ice.

3 Garnish with passion fruit wheel and a squeeze of passion fruit pulp on top plus a lime spiral.

After-dinner & Shooter Cocktails

The after-dinner drinks are of a digestive type served after lunch, dinner or early in the evening. The taste and quality is usually rich and sweet, and they can be served hot or cold. The shooters are minuscule cocktails served throughout the day and night. They consist of straight, chilled flavoured spirits or various flavoured liqueurs floated on top of each other in a layered fashion.

ESPRESSO MARTINI

Rumour has it that Dick Bradsell of the Soho Brasserie, London was asked, in 1983, by one of his customers to 'make a drink to wake her up', and the result was this popular, rich cocktail.

3.5cl vodka, 1.5cl Kahlúa liqueur, sugars syrup (according to individual preference of sweetness) 1 short strong espresso (30ml, made from good-quality coffee)

1 Add all the ingredients to a cocktail shaker with ice, shake briskly.
2 Strain into a chilled double cocktail glass.
3 Garnish with 3 edible coffee beans or pinch of chocolate or cinnamon (optional).

IRISH COFFEE

Created by Joe Sheridan, Foynes Airport, Limerick, in 1942, this after-dinner cocktail was internationally popularised by *San Francisco Chronicle* columnist Stanton Delaplane. Can be served on its own, or with shortbread cookies as a desert.

4cl Irish whiskey, 9cl hot coffee, 3cl fresh cream, 1 tsp of brown sugar

1 Warm the Irish whiskey over a burner (if possible) and add to a heat-resistant glass.
2 Add the coffee and brown sugar and stir.
3 Float fresh, lightly whipped cream on top, Do not re-stir.

Variations:
Calypso Coffee: Tia Maria liqueur; Caribbean/Jamaican Coffee: Dark rum; Café Royale: Cognac or Brandy; Italian Coffee: Strega or Amaretto liqueur; Nutty Irishman: Frangelico liqueur and Irish Cream liqueur; Prince Charles Coffee: Drambuie liqueur.

Espresso Martini.

Irish Coffee.

 Scan the code for a demonstration on making an Espresso Martini.

THE TAX COLLECTOR

This cocktail was created by DIT bar studies student Trudy Matthews, Harry's On the Green, Dublin, 2015.

5cl Dictador 12 Years Solera System Rum, 1cl sugar syrup, 2 dashes Angostura bitters, 1 dash Aztec Chocolate bitters

1 Pour all ingredients into a mixing glass with ice and stir (3 minutes minimum).
2 Strain into a chilled old-fashioned glass with ice.
3 Garnish with fresh orange peel.

VALLEY OF FIRE

Inspired by the vista and contrasting lush vegetation at the Valley of Fire, Nevada's oldest state park, lecturer Frank Cullen created this cocktail, which went on to win the 1990 Bols Cocktail Challenge, held in Dublin.

6cl pineapple juice, 1cl grenadine syrup, 2.5cl Crème de Banane liqueur, 5cl Tequila Silver, 1cl Midori (Melon) liqueur, fresh cream (lightly whipped)

1 Add all the ingredients (except the cream and Midori) to a cocktail shaker with ice, shake briskly.
2 Strain into a highball glass with ice.
3 Pour the Midori (over a teaspoon) down the inside of the glass; it will settle on the bottom of the glass.
4 Garnish with strawberry, pineapple leaf, or kiwi.
5 Float the semi-whipped cream on top of the cocktail by pouring it carefully over a bar spoon. Sprinkle with chocolate flakes.

B-52

Taking its name from the US B-52 Stratofortress bomber, this multi-layered minuscule cocktail, created in Alice's Restaurant, Malibu, in the 1960s, has many variations, referred to as the B-50 series.

2cl Kahlúa Coffee liqueur, 2cl Bailey's Irish Cream liqueur, 2cl Grand Marnier liqueur

1 Select a cool, small shot glass.
2 Layer the ingredients in order (by pouring slowly over the back of a teaspoon).
3 Serve carefully to keep the layers separate.

Variations
B-51: substitute Frangelico liqueur for Grand Marnier; B-53: substitute Sambuca liqueur for Bailey's; B-54: substitute Amaretto liqueur for Grand Marnier; B-55: substitute absinthe for Grand Marnier.

HOT SHOT

Created in Sweden in 1989, the combined flavours of this mini winter warmer are delicious and dazzling. Try to keep the layers separate for the visual effect of this clever cocktail.

1cl Galliano liqueur, 1cl coffee (hot), 1cl cream (lightly whipped)

1 Select a small (room temperature) shot glass.
2 Carefully layer the ingredients listed above, in the order listed, over the back of a small spoon.
3 Advise your guests to consume in one swallow to obtain the combined flavour delivery.

Valley of Fire.

B-52.

Alcohol-free Cocktails

Alcohol-free long-drink cocktails are served throughout the day, and often contain restorative ingredients. They consist of juices, fruits, vegetables, syrups and lemonades. The taste and quality is usually medium to neutral in flavour (sometimes a little sweet).

ELDERFLOWER AND MINT LEMONADE

A thirst-quenching cocktail which can be enjoyed throughout the day.

6-8 mint leaves, 3cl lemon juice, 1.75cl elderflower cordial, 5ml sugar syrup, soda water

1 Add all ingredients (except soda) to a cocktail shaker and shake with ice.
2 Strain into an ice-filled Collins or Hurricane glass and top with soda water.
3 Garnish with mint sprigs (on the stalk) and add straws.

MINT TEA MISCHIEF

Created by DIT bar studies student Daniel Tinsley, Fallons Gastro Pub, Naas Road, Kilcullen, this cocktail won the 2015 Third Monin Cocktail Challenge in Dublin.

1cl Monin Sugar Syrup, 1.5cl Monin Lemongrass Syrup, 12.4cl Twinings strawberry and raspberry herbal tea, 5-7 mint leaves

1 Shake all ingredients with ice in a cocktail shaker.
2 Strain into an ice-filled jar glass.
3 Garnish with sprig of mint, strawberry and short straws.

NICKIE NOGGY NOO

This after-dinner treat was created by DIT cocktail studies student Nickie Connolly, Jo'Burger Restaurant, Castlemarket, Dublin, 2015.

2cl of pistachio syrup, 1.5cl cardamom syrup, 6cl milk, 2cl fresh cream, egg white

1 Shake all ingredients with ice in a cocktail shaker.
2 Strain into a chilled old fashioned glass with some ice.
3 Garnish with a sprinkle of chopped pistachios, grated lime zest and lime swirl.

VIRGIN MULE

A delicious and refreshing cocktail that offers so much flavour; key to the drink is the non-alcoholic ginger beer which is much more gingery and spicy than ginger ale.

3cl lime juice, 1.75cl sugar syrup, ice cubes, ginger beer

1 Shake all ingredients (except ginger beer) with ice in a cocktail shaker.
2 Strain into a tall glass with ice and top with ginger beer.
3 Garnish with a wedge of fresh lime.

Elderflower and Mint Lemonade.

Mint Tea Mischief.

Nickie Noggy Noo.

Virgin Mule.

ENTERTAINING

Dining at Home

Being a host, especially for those special occasions, can be daunting. A few tips can help the host relax and enjoy the experience, as well as the guests.

For those who do not entertain regularly, it is a good idea not to be too ambitious with your menu. Take a step back and do some basic planning. Make a list of everything you will need for your event. Give yourself enough time to set the dining-room table, prepare the cutlery, glasses, delph or organise the room where you plan to entertain. Consider the type of dishes you plan to serve and whether you need some of these to be prepared in advance.

Foods like soups, casseroles, and starters such as Ham Hock Terrine with Pickled Vegetables or desserts such as Homemade Spiced Apple Pie or Raspberry & Lemon Curd Pavlova can all be prepared ahead of time. Cooking your food in front of your guests can be stressful and you could miss out on being part of the party. However, for the more advanced home chef, cooking food to order, such as Celtic Steak or Dublin Bay Prawns with Pernod or desserts such as Michel Roux's Soufflé au Chocolat, brings freshness and creativity to the overall experience.

Entertaining at home is not always just about the food. Little professional touches such as serving hot food on hot plates and not overfilling plates but keeping seconds in the middle of the table all add to the occasion.

Setting the atmosphere can be a part of the overall entertainment. Think about the lighting; is it too bright or dark? Simple tweaks like lighting a candle, or a fire, can create the right ambience. If you are sitting down to dine, the table setting needs some thought. A round table works well, allowing all guests to see and talk to each other. If you don't have a round table, it is a good idea to seat guests at both ends of the table.

Christmastime is when many of us entertain. The table setting lends atmosphere to a special occasion.

A romantic setting for two.

Choose your cutlery, glasses and delph to suit the occasion, if possible; crisp folded napkins can be one of those extra touches. Any table centrepiece should be low so that all guests can see each other around the table. An interesting table centrepiece can also be a good talking point or ice-breaker. Your guests will notice and appreciate your efforts.

Finally, cleaning as you go will take the pressure off the big clean-up at the end of the night and will not be so distracting either for you or your guests.

When in doubt: do simple things and do them well, and have a good selection of drinks available!

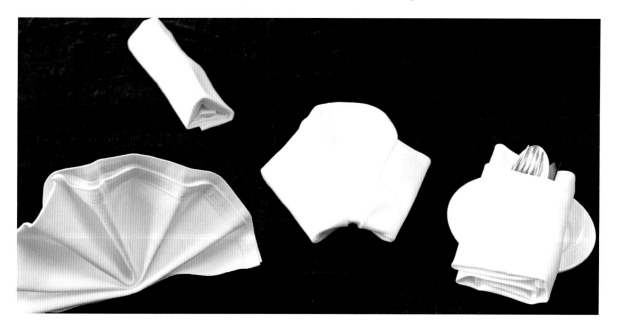

Cleverly folded napkins add a professional touch to the table.
For tips on table setting and napkin folding scan the code bottom right.

Matching Food & Drink

The 'meal' is one of life's most significant rituals and also one of its great pleasures. It not only comforts and nourishes, it also brings us together and enriches our relationships. Equally one of Ireland's traditional pillars of hospitality is in offering a drink to guests; whether it is a glass of refreshing water, a warming tea, a nip of whiskey or the finest wine to toast an occasion. When entertaining at home, we seek to provide our guests with the best, but often the key to successful entertaining is to keep it simple. Your guests are already delighted to have been invited and not to have any washing-up to do!

Matching food and wine is much easier than many of us think. Although often good quality mineral water works perfectly well with many foods, as it is neutral and refreshes the palate, there are many of us that really do love a glass of wine. Below are some simple guidelines to enhance the overall experience.

FOOD & WINE

Food and wine are gastronomically linked – socially, physically and spiritually. Food and wine are ever evolving with some classic pairings coming and going while others have remained in vogue. It is important to know (and maybe challenge) the tried and tested traditional pairings, but we can broaden our horizons and discover new pairings. Looking at the recent resurgence of sherry, the dry fortified wines of Jerez in Southern Spain, these wines have emerged as stunning matches for all sorts of exciting world foods, especially Japanese cuisine. Dry sherries (not the cream sherries we know of old) have a special umami character and this pairs seamlessly with non-spicy Asian foods such as sushi, seaweeds, miso and other fermented dishes. When you discover a good combination that is new to you it can be a revelation and your overall knowledge and appreciation of food and wine matching becomes clearer and stronger as you see what works well.

GLASSWARE & SERVING

We can influence how wine tastes by serving correctly.

One of the most common mistakes made both at

Wine glasses should have brilliant clarity, good balance, a fine rim; it is best not to use coloured glasses.

home and in industry is serving wine at the wrong temperature. Frustratingly, red wines are often served too warm and whites mouth numbingly cold. If red wine is served too warm, the flavour becomes muddy and the taste of the alcohol dominates while masking the fruit. With white wine, if it is served too cold, it can lack flavour and nuance, though it will be refreshing. The matching chart at the end of this chapter details some appropriate serving temperatures for wines and other beverages.

THE BASICS TO KEEP IN MIND

1 All wines contain acid and natural sugar in varying quantities. The acid is vital as it helps to balance the sugar in wine and it gives it drinkability and freshness. Use the acid found in grapes such as Chardonnay, Riesling, Sangiovese or Pinot Noir to cut through rich foods that have higher fat content, eg meats, cheeses or pâté.

2 Be careful to avoid matching wines that are naturally acidic with foods of the same nature as this can clash – vinaigrettes on salad combined with say a zingy Sauvignon Blanc could be problematic.

3 To get a good food/wine combination we are not looking for foods that taste the same as our wine. We really want wine that complements the food by adding another

A useful piece of wine kit is a decanter. It shows off a wine beautifully and improves the flavour of older vintage wines.

dimension, usually a cleansing and/or enriching character.

4 Don't always focus on the protein or main component of the dish, ie the meat or the fish or vegetable; alternatively look at what are the accompaniments to this. Often the sauce, garnish or dressings are the lead flavours and the ones that take the meat or fish in a certain direction. If you can match a wine to those flavours then you are also in the right direction.

5 Balance is the key word. Try to get a sense of the weight and texture of the food in the dish. If the food is delicate and light, a ripe and full Argentinian Malbec may not be the best option and a fresher lighter red from a cooler climate may complement it far better.

Wine remains ever popular as a partner for food.

FINAL TIPS

Try to think of the wine you are going to serve as though it is an ingredient or the final seasoning to the food. Focus on the texture(s) and temperature of the food. Who are you serving it to? The serving environment:

is it summer or winter; a heated room or an outdoor terrace? The balance of acids, sugars and flavours is key to successful food and wine pairing; experimenting and discovering is the fun part. Consider also that very expensive or special bottle of wine that you have been saving; it may not be the right wine for the food and could actually end up being a disappointment. If you do decide that you want to open it, then be sure to buy the ingredients that match.

A selection of craft beers from Carlow Brewing Company.

FOOD LOVES BEER

Beer behaves differently from wine when it comes to matching it with food. Beers lack acidity and tannin, two qualities that help wine match food well. But they have other qualities such as bitterness, sweetness, carbonation, lower levels of alcohol and, most importantly, a range of flavours you do not find in wine (chocolate, smoke and caramel etc.) that more than compensate.

The most significant of those is bitterness. There are two types of bitterness, hop bitterness and roasted malt bitterness. Hop bitterness works well with spices, which is why IPAs are such a great match for spicy food, while roasted malt bitterness has a palate-cleansing quality which can help with foods such as roast or barbecued meats, cheese and chocolate. With a rich chocolate dessert, for example, you don't want yet more richness in your glass. You want something that is going to be refreshing like a bitter porter or a sour wheat beer. When it comes to matching food and beer, there are some basic considerations to take into account.

1 *Complement or contrast:* It is a question of balance. If you know the flavours are going to be delicate, like a salad or a seafood risotto, you want a beer that will not overwhelm them, such as a pilsner (Moretti, Sol, Samuel Adams) or a wheat beer (O'Hara's Curim, Erdinger, Paulaner). If the flavours are full, as they would be in a steak and ale pie or a beef stew, you want a beer of equal weight, like a modern Irish red ale (O'Hara's Irish Red, see right) or Irish stout (Guinness, Murphy's). If the flavours are extreme – very hot, spicy or sweet – you want a beer that offers some respite and refreshment.

2 *The order:* In general, it is better to drink lighter, drier beers before richer, sweeter, more powerful ones, just as you serve lighter dishes before more intensely flavoured foods.

3 *Carbonation:* This is more pronounced in some beers like wheat beers or pilsners than in others such as traditional Irish ales, and virtually non-existent in other beers. Carbonated drinks support flavours better than still ones. The carbonation of a cherry-flavoured Lambic (try Timmermans), on the

other hand, will preserve the fruit flavours of the beer, cleansing the palate between each mouthful and echoing but not overwhelming those of the dessert. It means you can rely on flavour rather than strength or sweetness for the match, which again makes for a more refreshing experience.

4 *Light or dark:* A light or dark colour does not necessarily indicate a light or powerful beer as an O'Hara Amber Adventure, from the Carlow Brewing Company or a Coalface Black IPA, from Carrig Brewing in Leitrim will testify. Let flavour rather than colour be your guide.

FINAL TIPS

Aim to avoid the flavour of the beer overwhelming the dish, or vice versa. Although beer goes well with many cheeses, some of the stronger versions will drown any good beer. Similarly, a strong, vinegar-based salad dressing, high in acid, will interfere with even a highly malted brew. For further suggestions on food and beer pairings see the Matching Chart (p200).

Below: German Black Lager Beer, Köstritzer, is mahogany in colour with a creamy head and exudes spicy rich aromas of roasted chestnuts, dark honey, bitter chocolate and fresh baked bread. Malty rich flavours continue on tasting, with rich coffee and chocolate balanced by a dry bitter-sweet finish. This complex dark lager complements dark, roasted or barbecued meats, including steak, game and sausages, and yet surprisingly it has a cleansing, light finish, as with most lagers, and is ideal for cleansing the palate of rich, robust flavours.

Matching Chart for Food & Drinks

Dishes & Ingredients	Classic/Contemporary Wine Pairing	Beer Pairing/Other Suggestions	Avoid
Starters/Fish Dishes			
Oysters, clam, shrimp, lobster	**Classic:** Chablis; Champagne; Sauvignon Blanc. **Contemporary:** Manzanilla or Fino sherry; Aged Muscadet; chilled light-bodied reds.	Entre Deux Mers; Trebbiano di Lugano; Sake. Pilsner lagers (hop presence and CO2 levels do not overpower the delicate flavours).	Sweet or fruity wine; tannic wine.
Oily fish	**Classic:** Champagne; unoaked Chardonnay; Muscadet; Vinho Verde. **Contemporary:** Albariño; High-quality sparkling water; smoky tea such as Lapsang Souchong.	Manzanilla sherry; Sauvignon Blanc; dry cider.	Tannic red or high-alcohol wine.
Buffalo wings		Pale ale/IPA (beer bitterness contrasts the dish sweetness).	
Crabs and scallops	**Classic:** Riesling; Chardonnay; Burgundy White; Champagne. **Contemporary:** Dry German Riesling; Chenin Blanc.	Fino sherry; Pinot Gris; delicate teas; pilsner lagers.	Red wine.
Calamari		Pilsner lagers (both food and drink are light and crisp).	
Fat fish (salmon or tuna)		Pilsner lagers (strong hoppy aromas pair well with these fish dishes).	
Prawns or tofu		Pale lagers (pair well with these lighter starters).	
White fish	**Classic:** Chardonnay; Pinot Grigio. **Contemporary:** Semillon; Albariño; Sauvignon Blanc.	Green tea; dry sherry (fried fish).	Tannic or oaky wine.
Sushi		Light lager (sushi and the lager are both light and crisp).	
Smoked fish	.	Pale ale (complements smoky flavours perfectly).	
Salads			
Salad with citrus vinaigrette		Wheat beer (light, pleasing with salad).	
Salad with raspberry vinaigrette		Lambic raspberry beer (light with complementary flavours).	

Main Courses			
Game meats and birds	**Classic:** Côte-Rôtie; Syrah; Pinot Noir. **Contemporary:** Priorat; Gevrey Chambertin; Oloroso sherry.	Mencia; Douro. Steam or amber ale (fruity dark ale for stronger game).	Acidic white; very tannic wine.
Roast beef	**Classic:** Cabernet; Red Burgundy. **Contemporary:** Languedoc Red; Bandol; Cahors.	Malbec; Rioja; Xinomavro; Barolo. Belgian beers.	Acidic white.
Steak/well-done beef		Irish stout; red ale; traditional English bitter.	
Roast leg of lamb	**Classic:** St Emilion (Bordeaux); Rioja (Reserva/Gran Reserva). **Contemporary:** Ribero Del Duero; Chinon; Cabernet Sauvignon; Shiraz.	Shiraz; Pinotage; Zinfandel. Porters (rich, dark, malt variety, with notes of coffee).	Acidic white.
Lamb (rack)		Syrah, Bordeaux, Barolo or pale ale (fruitiness pairs well).	
Chicken/turkey	**Classic:** Oaked Chardonnay (Roast); Pinot Noir. **Contemporary:** Beaujolais.	Dolcetto; sparkling wine (fried chicken); pale ale (a delightful contrast).	Sweet wine; tannic red wine.
Pork	**Classic:** Pinot Noir, Côtes du Rhone Villages. **Contemporary:** N. Rhone – Crozes Hermitage, Chianti Classico.	Depends on the fat content of the pork. Irish red ale or Helles Lager (if high fat content); cider (lean pork dish).	
Chicken Satay or Cashew Chicken		Brown ale (complements the dish nuttiness).	
Curries, spiced foods, stew, goulash	**Classic:** Off-dry Riesling; Gewürztraminer. **Contemporary:** Tea; Kefir; Lasse; Ayran; Viognier.	Zinfandel; Pinot Gris; dark lagers (cut heaviness of the sauces).	High-alcohol; tannic wine.
Pasta (the sauce is the key factor)	**Classic:** In general, Chianti Classico or Barbera for a meaty or tomato-based sauce. **Contemporary:** Chardonnay; Frascati; Vermentino (with creamy pasta).	Verdicchio or Barolo with mushroom or truffle pasta.	Tannic wine with tomato or spicy sauces.
Tapas	**Classic:** Dry sherry. **Contemporary:** Cava; Albariño.	Champagne; rosé wine. Crisp beers (eg pilsners).	
Pizza		Lagers/Pale ale (established pairing).	
Barbecue		Porter (complementary sweet flavours with roasted and caramel undertones).	

Burger		IPA or Irish stout (bitterness of these beers balances the heaviness of dish as well as the umami flavour).	
Desserts			
Vanilla ice cream		Chocolate stout (complementary flavours).	
Pumpkin pie		Belgian Abbey Beer (complementary caramel flavours and richness).	
Chocolate cake or Torte		Imperial Stout. Complementary flavours and similar richness.	
Sweet chocolate desserts		Barley wine beer (an ideal combination).	
Rich chocolate desserts		Belgian Trappist dark ales/oatmeal stout/ Scotch Ale (complement rich flavours).	
Fresh fruit salads - raspberries or cherries		Lambic beers (especially fruit-flavoured).	
Cheese			
Cheese (general)	**Classic:** Off-dry wine; Port Wine; Pinot Noir; Riesling. **Contemporary:** Barolo; Champagne; Amontillado Sherry; Gewürztraminer.	Sauternes with blue cheese; Vin Jaune with Comte.	Cheese is so varied. There are many options. Experiment!
Soft Cheeses (cream, ricotta, goat)	**Classic:** Sancerre; Sauvignon Blanc. **Contemporary:** Albariño; Champagne.	Wheat beer.	Rich red wine.
Cheddar	Cheese is so varied. There are many options. Experiment!	Double bock or a fruity ale.	
Hard cheeses (eg Parmigiano), Roquefort		Porter or barley wine beer.	
Strong-flavoured cheese		Barley wine beer.	

Note: In this chart some pairings suggest specific wine regions while others broadly suggest the grape varietal. The old tropes of white wine with fish or chicken and red wine with beef or lamb are outdated. The best beverage and food pairings are what works for you. But a tip for success might be to match the extra components of the dish (garnishes, sauces or strong flavours) and not the actual protein. Try to avoid: (a) acidic items such as vinaigrette or pickled food with very acidic wine, (b) tannic red wine with spicy or Asian food, especially chilli, (c) heavy sweet desserts with very sweet wine.

THE FUTURE OF FOOD

Food in Ireland

As a nation of food lovers with increasingly adventurous and discerning tastes, it is interesting to note the various factors that contribute to the success of Ireland's food offering. Here we take a look at food trends, marketing, healthy eating, sustainability, molecular gastronomy and the growth of Ireland's food markets.

FOOD TRENDS

Ireland has become one of the food hot spots in the world. Ireland's agri-food industry accounts for 8% of GDP and a similar proportion of total employment, amounting to almost 160,000 jobs. Our export value has the potential to grow to €19bn per annum by 2025.

Our young, well-educated and increasingly diverse population is having an impact on the food industry. Lifestyle changes have led to changes in where and how we consume our food. The 'casualisation' of dining and the rise of 'snacking', street food, upmarket fast food, dashboard dining and quality casual restaurants and pubs have added different options to our dining experience, opening the way for new opportunities and product innovation within the food industry.

MARKETING

Marketing has a key role to play in the success of Ireland's food and hospitality sector. Consumers respond positively to seeing the human face and the story behind a product. This bodes well for the small craft and artisan producers as they have a personal story which can help bring the provenance and quality of their product to the fore. High-quality, authentic, Irish ingredients that create a unique flavour as well

Gourmet puy lentil and mushroom burger, a delicious vegetarian alternative to a red-meat burger.

as traditional recipes that share a history form part of a popular trend. Brands, however, need their unique selling proposition; this could be the chefs' reputation, company ethos, stand-out packaging or memorable logo design (or a combination of these), but, behind it all, the product or service must be supreme, aimed squarely at its target customers. The era of the 'celebrity' chef continues, and their associated brand identities and media profiles are central to their success.

SOCIAL MEDIA

Food producers, large and small, are aware that the old techniques encompassing print and broadcast media have been joined by social media, such as Instagram, Twitter, Snapchat, Facebook, Apps and YouTube, not to mention the phenomenon that is food blogging. However, the human element should not be underestimated. Traditional Irish hospitality, our world-renowned '*fáilte*' remains a unique selling proposition.

SUPPORT FOR FOOD ENTREPRENEURS

Ireland continues to support the food entrepreneur. The Local Enterprise Office (LEO) offers valuable support, investment, training and mentoring for those interested in starting any business, including food. Joining forces with Bord Bia and SuperValu, the LEO has set up the 'Food Academy' to support artisan food producers throughout Ireland. The Food Academy has engaged with over 500 producers. Another programme, 'Food Works', a collaboration between Enterprise Ireland, Bord Bia and Teagasc, has supported over 60 new food companies. Enterprise Ireland also offers a number of early-stage financial supports such as the Competitive Start Fund, the Innovation Voucher or New Frontiers.

HEALTHY EATING

Food entrepreneurs also need to take into account nutrition and healthy eating. A healthy, balanced diet and lifestyle are vital for our physical and emotional wellbeing, even more so as obesity is now a serious issue in Irish society. The drive to educate people about food and healthy eating is leading to an increased awareness of the ingredients used in processed foods and how to maintain a healthy balanced diet. Food companies need to consider the raw materials in their products and the health impacts of all their ingredients. Dishes should be formulated in such a way that the nutritional content is of high value and fat and salt levels are reduced, along with the removal of chemical additives.

The typical Western diet, ie processed, calorie-dense, high in unhealthy fats, sugars and salt and low in fibre, has been linked with the development of many diseases. These include obesity, type 2 diabetes, heart disease and stroke, bowel problems, cancers, bone and joint disorders, and mental health disorders. Inactivity, stress, smoking and consumption of excessive alcohol exacerbate these disorders. Healthy eating however does not and should not mean depriving oneself of foods which you enjoy or strict limitations to a diet or indeed excessive supplement use. In fact, simple changes to our diet and lifestyle can make significant differences to our health and wellbeing.

Eating vegetables in season has long been a French cuisine tradition and is still one of the best ways to eat fresh, locally produced foods.

SOME SIMPLE TIPS TO HELP ACHIEVE A HEALTHY DIET ARE:

EAT SLOWLY: It takes time for your brain to receive the message that the stomach if full. Eating quickly, you are more likely to eat more.

READ FOOD LABELS: Know the ingredient list. Producers normally list ingredients in descending order by weight. The first ingredient listed contributes the largest amount and the last ingredient listed contributes the least to the product.

Understanding the nutrition panel allows you to compare similar products. Consumers should look at the 'per 100g' column: low fat is 3g of fat or less per 100g, high fat is 20g of fat or more per 100g; low sugar is less than 5g of sugar per 100g, high sugar is more than 15g of sugar per 100g; low salt is 0.3g salt per 100g, high salt is 1.5g salt per 100g.

SWITCH YOUR SOURCE OF FATS: Switch from confectionery, take-away and processed food that are high in saturated and unhealthy trans fats to healthy fats such as olive oil, corn oil, rapeseed oil, fish, avocados, nuts and seeds, high in mono and polyunsaturated fats (these are still calorie-rich so the amount used should be measured).

SWITCH FROM WHITE (REFINED) TO BROWN (UNREFINED/COMPLEX) CEREALS: Brown rice, pasta and low-sugar wholegrain breads are rich in fibre, vitamins and minerals and keep you fuller for longer.

COLOUR IS THE SPICE OF LIFE: Eat more fruit and vegetables, use a variety of colours, make homemade, low-fat, smoothies if you find fruit and vegetables difficult to consume.

Many believe that the more colours that appear on the plate, the better the balance of nutrients.

CONTROL PORTION SIZE: Use a smaller plate. Half your plate should be vegetables/salad with the other half divided in two, half being carbohydrates, eg brown rice; half being protein, eg lean meat or fish. As a guide, a 200ml disposable plastic cup is 1 portion of cooked rice or pasta, and ½ a 200ml disposable plastic cup is 1 portion of cooked vegetables, 2 small fruit (eg kiwis) are 1 portion and 1 medium apple is a portion.

EAT MORE FISH: In particular oily fish (twice a week), eg salmon, mackerel, sardines and tuna.

DRINK MORE WATER: Instead of fruit juices and caffeinated drinks.

INVEST IN A NON-STICK COOKING PAN: Do not add oil to the pan when cooking mince or other fat rich foods. Drain off this fat. Measure the amount of oil you add to a pan, eg a teaspoon of oil contains approximately 45 calories and a teaspoon of butter contains approximately 37 calories. Some of the healthy food trends anticipated over the next couple of years:

VEGETABLE CRISPS: Crisps made from vegetables make a healthier treat. Beetroot, parsnip, celeriac and sweet potato all make great alternatives to the potato crisp. Leafy green vegetables, including the superfood 'kale', are also a healthy snack food.

FERMENTED FOODS AND DRINKS: Many consumers are focusing on improving their digestive system. This demand is resulting in the growth of gluten-free foods and probiotics. People are also considering fermented foods as another way to improve their health. Products like sauerkraut, pickles, kimchi and fermented vegetable drinks are available.

Dairy- and gluten-free, high-protein ice cream.

MOLECULAR GASTRONOMY

Allied to the healthy-eating perspective is Molecular Gastronomy. A key question most food providers ask themselves is: how can food dishes and products be made more exciting and inviting for the customer? One way is through Molecular Gastronomy, which is allowing for the creation of innovative dishes and drinks.

Molecular Gastronomy concerns what happens and why it happens during the preparation and cooking of food. Applications of Molecular Gastronomy include 'Molecular Cooking' and 'Note-by-Note Cooking'. The former uses ingredients and equipment associated with scientific laboratories. Chefs use liquid nitrogen to create fresh tasting and super smooth ice cream, made at your table in the midst of a theatrical smoky atmosphere. Why is the quality of the ice cream superior? It is all down to the smaller-sized ice crystals.

'Note-by-Note Cooking' is based on the creation of dishes that are made entirely from compounds and do not use any meat, fish, vegetables or fruits. The chef has a blank canvas to design the shapes of the various parts of the dish, the colours, tastes, odours, temperatures, trigeminal stimulation, consistency, and nutritional aspects.

The food industry has recognised the importance of Molecular Gastronomy and the role of culinary arts in the development of tasty, enjoyable and well-presented foods. Having a chef/food scientist (concept or development chef) working in food production is one development required to meet some of the demands for sustainable, tasty and wholesome food products for the future.

SUSTAINABILITY

Globally the population is set to grow from 7.3 billion in 2015 to 8.5 billion in 2030 and 9 billion by 2050, so the demand for food is continuously growing. This creates an enormous pressure on agricultural land, water and other natural resources. Therefore, the issue of sustainable food continues to gather momentum. But what does it mean?

With no agreed legal definition, there is a lot of confusion about what food sustainability really is and why it is so important. It encompasses a wide range of issues: use of agricultural land, human health and safety, animal welfare, water availability, economics, affordability or a strong food industry. For some it is about being able to feed the world.

The story surrounding the food supply chain and with the food on our plate is a complicated one. Understanding and addressing sustainability and environmental issues requires world leaders, governments, food companies, chefs, scientists and policy makers to work together to develop and implement long-term strategies.

Within the School of Culinary Arts and Food Technology we educate our students about Ireland's food sustainability and growth, paying particular attention to the provenance of ingredients. The aim is for students to understand the importance of knowing where the food comes from (the raw materials and the suppliers) and for them to understand how to educate the customer about the traceability of the product. Making our students aware of how to reduce waste and minimise environmental damage is also a key part of our syllabi; food companies that supply our School are exploring new ideas and are working as partners to achieve this sustainability.

Examples of such Irish companies include Manor Farm and Country Crest, who work closely together to reduce carbon emissions through cutting down on transport, eg Country Crest locate Manor Farm's chicken farms on their land. The chicks are thereby fed with the grain grown on the land and in turn the chicks' waste is used to nurture the land for the food and vast range of vegetables produced by Country Crest.

Apart from these large producers, indigenous 'craft' and 'artisan' producers have also become a familiar sight in our communities, displaying the best of locally grown produce.

GROWTH OF IRELAND'S FOOD MARKETS

Bord Bia research has identified over 150 diverse food markets in Ireland, including community markets, farmers markets, lunch-time markets, weekend city markets, co-operatives and country markets. They largely share the same aim, which is to allow producers to sell their (usually local) produce directly to consumers in a traditional market environment. Although this sense of connection with the community remains important, the markets have evolved and producers are not necessarily from the local area, but participate because they are either producing themselves or sourcing directly from another region.

ANYONE FOR CRICKET?

Using insects as a sustainable source of food in the Western regions is also of interest in terms of food sustainability. With the increased global demand for food and the negative impact that its production can have on the environment, eg land and water pollution

High energy protein bar incorporating cricket flour.

and the emission of greenhouse gases contributing to climate change, alternative solutions are needed. In the School of Culinary Arts and Food Technology, we are investigating the increasing trend in the Western world of using edible insects as sources of food and animal feed for the future.

More than 2 billion people consume insects as part of their diet in parts of Asia, Africa and Latin America. The most commonly consumed insects are beetles, caterpillars, bees, wasps and ants. Others include grasshoppers, locusts and crickets. Many of these edible insects contain high quality protein, vitamins and amino acids.

Chefs across the globe are already placing insects on their menus. Britain's first insect restaurant, Grub Kitchen, was opened in 2015, in Pembrokeshire, Wales. According to Head Chef, Andy Holcroft, the opening of his restaurant will be a step towards normalising insect consumption in the UK. He has developed many insect dishes, including the restaurant's signature bug burger (a blend of toasted crickets, mealworms and grasshopper mixed with spinach, sundried tomato and seasoning) with polenta chips and tatziki. Other menu items include a 'Bug Board' tasting board, with a selection of plain and seasoned insect treats, and for dessert, cricket, cardamon and carrot cake. Also in 2015, in his pop-up restaurant in Noma at Mandarin Oriental, Tokyo, top chef René Redzepi placed jumbo shrimp, seasoned with tiny black ants, on his menu, while Archipelago in London have served up chocolate-covered locusts and love bug salad.

LOOKING AHEAD

The past two decades have seen tremendous growth in the Irish food industry due to the establishment of a multitude of artisan food producers, increased excellence in restaurants and the rapid expansion of Irish food products into global markets. The future belongs to those with the vision, confidence and imagination to seek out and exploit new food opportunities.

The provision of such food leaders with the skills and flair to become entrepreneurs and trailblazers in Irelands food-service sector has been the *raison d'être* of Cathal Brugha Street for the last seventy-five years. The School of Culinary Arts and Food Technology will no doubt continue to be at the forefront of Ireland's thriving food industry.

Conversion Charts

CONVERSION CHART: COMPARING OVEN THERMOSTATS
MARKED IN CELSIUS TO FAHRENHEIT WITH GAS MARKS

CELSIUS	FAHRENHEIT	GAS MARKS	CELSIUS	FAHRENHEIT	GAS MARKS
290	550		170	325	3
270	525		150	300	2
250	500		140	275	1
240	475	9	130	250	1/2
230	450	8	110	225	1/4
220	425	7	100	200	Low
200	400	6	80	175	
190	375	5	70	150	
180	350	4			

NB: These are dial markings and not exact conversions.

CONVERSION CHART: CONVERTING RECIPES FROM IMPERIAL TO METRIC MEASURES

Converting Grams			
Imperial measurement	Metric equivalent	Imperial measurement	Metric equivalent
1 oz	25 g	9 oz	250 g
2 oz	50 g	10 oz	275 g
3 oz	75 g	11 oz	300 g
4 oz	100-125 g	12 oz	350 g
5 oz	150 g	13 oz	375 g
6 oz	175 g	14 oz	400 g
7 oz	200 g	15 oz	425 g
8 oz	225 g	16 oz (1 lb)	450 g

Converting Millilitres			
Imperial measurement	Metric equivalent	Imperial measurement	Metric equivalent
1 fl oz	25 ml	15 fl oz (3/4 pint)	450 ml
2 fl oz	50 ml	20 fl oz (1 pint)	600 ml
5 fl oz	150 ml	35 fl oz	1 litre
10 fl oz (½ pint)	300 ml		

When you are measuring use this table for equivalents to convert recipes from imperial to metric measures or vice versa. Quantities are rounded-off to nearest values.

Glossary of Food Terms

Al dente: Italian term used to describe pasta that is cooked until it offers a slight resistance to the bite.

Barbecue: Generally used to refer to grilling done outdoors or over an open charcoal or wood fire. More specifically, barbecue refers to long, slow direct-heat cooking, including liberal basting with a barbecue sauce.

Baste: To moisten foods during cooking with pan drippings or special sauce to add flavour and prevent drying.

Batter: A mixture containing flour and liquid, thin enough to pour.

Beat: To mix rapidly in order to make a mixture smooth and light by incorporating as much air as possible.

Blanch: To immerse in rapidly boiling water and allow to cook slightly.

Blend: To incorporate two or more ingredients thoroughly.

Blind bake: (Sometimes called pre-baking). The process of pre-baking a pie crust (usually weighted down with dried beans) is necessary when it will be filled with an unbaked filling.

Boil: To heat a liquid until bubbles break continually on the surface.

Broil: To cook on a grill under strong, direct heat.

Caramelise: To heat sugar in order to turn it brown and give it a special taste.

Clarify: To separate and remove solids from a liquid, thus making it clear.

Cream: To soften a fat, especially butter, by beating it at room temperature. Butter and sugar are often creamed together, making a smooth, soft paste.

Cure: To preserve meats by drying and salting and/or smoking.

Deglaze: To dissolve the thin glaze of juices and brown bits on the surface of a pan in which food has been fried, sautéd or roasted. To do this, add liquid and stir and scrape over high heat, thereby adding flavour to the liquid for use as a sauce.

Degrease: To remove fat from the surface of stews, soups, or stock. Usually cooled in the refrigerator so that fat hardens and is easily removed.

Dice: To cut food in small cubes of uniform size and shape.

Dissolve: To cause a dry substance to pass into solution in a liquid.

Dredge: To sprinkle or coat with flour or other fine substance.

Drizzle: To sprinkle drops of liquid lightly over food in a casual manner.

Dust: To sprinkle food with dry ingredients. Use a strainer or a jar with a perforated cover, or try the good, old-fashioned way of shaking things together in a paper bag.

Fillet: As a verb, to remove the bones from meat or fish. A fillet is the piece of flesh after it has been boned.

Flake: To break lightly into small pieces.

Flambé: To flame foods by dousing in some form of potable alcohol and setting alight.

Fold: To incorporate a delicate substance, such as whipped cream or beaten egg whites, into another substance without releasing air bubbles. Cut down through mixture with spoon, whisk, or fork; go across bottom of bowl, up and over, close to surface. The process is repeated, while slowing rotating the bowl, until the ingredients are thoroughly blended.

Fricassee: To cook by braising; usually applied to fowl or rabbit.

Fry: To cook in hot fat. To cook in a lightly-greased pan is called pan-frying or sautéing; to cook in a one-to-two inch layer of hot fat is called shallow-fat frying; to cook in a deep layer of hot fat is called deep-fat frying.

Garnish: To decorate a dish or cocktail both to enhance its appearance and to provide a flavourful foil. Parsley, lemon slices, raw vegetables, chopped chives, and other herbs are all forms of garnishes.

Glaze: To cook with a thin sugar syrup cooked to crack stage; mixture may be thickened slightly. Also, to cover with a thin, glossy icing.

Grate: To rub on a grater that separates the food in various sizes of bits or shreds.

Gratin: From the French word for 'crust'. Term used to describe any oven-baked dish, usually cooked in a shallow oval gratin dish, on which a golden brown crust of bread crumbs, cheese or creamy sauce is formed.

Grill: To cook on a grill over intense heat.

Grind: To process solids by hand or mechanically to reduce them to tiny particles.

Julienne: To cut vegetables, fruits, or cheeses into thin strips.

Knead: To work and press dough with the palms of the hands or mechanically, to develop the gluten in the flour.

Lukewarm: Neither cool nor warm; approximately body temperature.

Marinate: To flavour and moisturise pieces of meat, poultry, seafood or vegetable by soaking them in or brushing them with a liquid mixture of seasonings known as a marinade. Dry marinade mixtures composed of salt, pepper, herbs or spices may also be rubbed into meat, poultry or seafood.

Meunière: Dredged with flour and sauteéd in butter.

Mince: To cut or chop food into extremely small pieces.

Mix: To combine ingredients, usually by stirring.

Pan-broil: To cook uncovered in a hot fry pan, pouring off fat as it accumulates.

Pan-fry: To cook in small amounts of fat.

Parboil: To boil until partially cooked; to blanch. Usually this procedure is followed by final cooking in a seasoned sauce.

Pare: To remove the outermost skin of a fruit or vegetable.

Peel: To remove the peels from vegetables or fruits.

Pickle: To preserve meats, vegetables, and fruits in brine.

Pinch: A pinch is the trifling amount you can hold between your thumb and forefinger.

Pit: To remove pits from fruits.

Planked: Cooked on a thick hardwood plank.

Plump: To soak dried fruits in liquid until they swell.

Poach: To cook very gently in hot liquid kept just below the boiling point.

Purée: To mash foods until perfectly smooth by hand, by rubbing through a sieve or food mill, or by whirling in a blender or food processor.

Quenelle: a rugby-ball-shaped scoop of ice cream, sorbet, whipped cream, crème fraiche, mousse etc.

Reduce: To boil down to reduce the volume.

Refresh: To run cold water over food that has been parboiled, to stop the cooking process quickly.

Render: To make solid fat into liquid by melting it slowly.

Roast: To cook by dry heat in an oven.

Sauté: To cook and/or brown food in a small amount of hot fat.

Scald: To bring to a temperature just below the boiling point.

Scallop: To bake a food, usually in a casserole, with sauce or other liquid. Crumbs often are sprinkled over.

Score: To cut narrow grooves or gashes partway through the outer surface of food.

Sear: To brown very quickly by intense heat. This method increases shrinkage but develops flavour and improves appearance.

Shred: To cut or tear in small, long, narrow pieces.

Sift: To put one or more dry ingredients through a sieve or sifter.

Simmer: To cook slowly in liquid over low heat at a temperature of about 180°C. The surface of the liquid should be barely moving, broken from time to time by slowly rising bubbles.

Skim: To remove impurities, whether scum or fat, from the surface of a liquid during cooking, thereby resulting in a clear, cleaner-tasting final product.

Steam: To cook in steam in a pressure cooker, deep well cooker, double boiler, or a steamer made by fitting a rack in a kettle with a tight cover. A small amount of boiling water is used, more water being added during steaming process, if necessary.

Steep: To extract colour, flavour, or other qualities from a substance by leaving it in water just below the boiling point.

Sterilise: To destroy micro-organisms by boiling, dry heat, or steam.

Stew: To simmer slowly in a small amount of liquid for a long time.

Stir: To mix ingredients with a circular motion until well blended or of uniform consistency.

Toss: To combine ingredients with a lifting motion.

Truss: To secure poultry with string or skewers, to hold its shape while cooking.

Whip: To beat rapidly to incorporate air and produce expansion, as in heavy cream or egg whites.

Index

Note: References to recipe illustrations are indicated by italics.